THREE GREEK PLAYS FOR THE THEATRE

EURIPIDES

Medea

Cyclops

ARISTOPHANES

The Frogs

Indiana University Press
Bloomington

Three GREEK
PLAYS *for the*
THEATRE

translated and edited by

PETER D. ARNOTT

for Catherine Mary

CONTENTS

FOREWORD

THE selection of the three plays appearing in this volume is not haphazard. First, they represent the three *genres* of Greek drama, tragedy, comedy and satyr play; second, they are connected by the personality of Euripides, who perhaps of all Greek playwrights has the greatest appeal for modern actors, audiences and readers. *Medea* and *Cyclops* show his skill in two very different drama forms; *The Frogs*, apart from its intrinsic merits as comedy, shows Euripides as others saw him, and satirizes many of his techniques and idiosyncracies.

When Euripides wrote, the Greek theatre was still a state-supported institution, financed out of public funds and forming part of a civic act of worship. This is not to say that theatre-going was a solemn affair. Audiences were noisy, lively and keenly critical, and would have been amused by the atmosphere of reverence which so often surrounds Greek plays in the modern theatre. It does mean, however, that performances were limited. Plays were given only at certain times of the year. In Athens dramatic festivals were held in honor of the god Dionysus, and it was in these festivals that the plays in this volume were first performed. Playwrights first submitted their manuscripts to the city magistrates for approval. Those accepted were performed in competition, and prizes were awarded for the best play and the best actor. The dramatist could normally expect only one performance of his work; *The Frogs*, which was repeated, is a rare exception. But this was still an amateur theatre, though amateur in the highest sense of the word. The dramatist did not expect to make a living from his works. It is only after the death of Euripides that the theatre becomes, in any real sense, commercial.

The plays were performed in open-air theatres, capable of accommodating the greater part of the population. In visualizing a Greek performance we must think not in terms of a modern playhouse but rather of a bull ring or football stadium; the audience, sitting on tiered seats rising steeply up the hill-side, virtually surrounded the performance and looked down on it from above. The playing area was chiefly given over to the *orchestra*, a circular arena where the chorus sang and danced. Behind this was a simple architectural façade which formed a permanent background for the plays. There was no attempt at scenic illusion. As in Shakespeare's theatre, the dramatist's words sufficed to set the scene. The virtues of this method are particularly apparent in comedy, where the action is not bound by the mechanics of scene changing but may shift location with a rapidity impossible in the illusionistic theatre. The dramatist secured his effects chiefly by words, music and choral spectacle.

o

Medea / EURIPIDES

INTRODUCTION

I. THE BACKGROUND

Medea was first produced in 431 B.C., and is the earliest of Euripides' extant tragedies, preceded only by the *Alcestis* (438). It appeared when Athens was at the height of her powers and seemingly impregnable. The calamitous war with Sparta was still to come. Euripides could still include in *Medea* a chorus celebrating the glories of Athens, a patriotic tribute such as the audiences loved. But the times were far from tranquil. Not only were the war-clouds gathering, but the city was passing through a period of profound spiritual and intellectual unrest, the consequences of which were to be no less far-reaching than those of the war itself. Criticism was rife. A new spirit of scientific enquiry was rapidly undermining the traditional religious beliefs. The Homeric picture of the gods as an enviable, though irresponsible, race of immortal aristocrats was rapidly yielding before a revaluation of man's place in the universe. Classes and discussions conducted by the sophists, professional teachers of philosophy, provided this growing spirit of dissatisfaction with a focal point. Here men learned to criticize conventional morality, and to question things which had for centuries been taken for granted.

It was easy to criticize the Olympic pantheon. It embodied no positive ethical code, and serious thinkers had long been alive to its deficiencies. Never before, however, had it been attacked so vehemently and so publicly. But it was not so easy to find something to put in its place. Much sophistic teaching was purely negative, demolishing the old ideas of religious and civic obligation and arguing that man's first duty was to himself; that laws were merely conventional agreements, in which self-interest was the only guiding principle. Together with this came a new interest in the art of rhetoric. Men learned to use and abuse the power of words. Skill in argument, the ability to speak on either side of a question with equal power and fluency, became an end in itself, and unscrupulous teachers exploited this tendency for their own profit.

The theatre, always sensitive to the slightest change of mood in the larger world outside, faithfully mirrors all these movements. Sophocles stands out as an advocate of humanism, a champion of man with all his faults and limitations. Euripides' technique is more destructive. He presses the claims of rationalism, and is the declared enemy of all loose and uncritical thinking. His method is to analyse the traditional myths, without mercy, in purely human terms, a process which makes their weaknesses glaringly apparent. While alive to the dangers of sophistry—Medea's reply to Jason (ll. 546 ff.) is a succinct condemnation of its worst abuses—he employs many of its techniques.

2. THE LEGEND

EURIPIDES bases this play on an apparently innocuous story, that of Jason, half-brother of King Pelias of Iolkos, who was ordered to prove his right to inherit the kingdom by recovering the fabulous Golden Fleece from the land of Colchis, in what is now the Black Sea. He sailed with a band of companions in a magic ship, the Argo, but arriving at Colchis found the Fleece guarded by apparently insuperable hazards, notably an ever-watchful dragon. He was aided, however, by Medea, princess of Colchis and a sorceress, who fell in love with him and used her magic powers to ensure his success. They escaped together, Medea killing and dismembering her young brother Apsurtos to delay pursuit. Back in Iolkos, and faced with the continuing hostility of King Pelias, Medea contrived his death by persuading the daughters of Pelias to boil him in a cauldron, a process which she claimed would restore his youth.

This was the generally accepted version of the legend so

far, and Euripides could take his audience's knowledge of it for granted. It forms the essential background to the present play, and is constantly referred to. The immediate action, however, is concerned with the sequel, about which there seems to have been far less agreement. After leaving Iolkos, Medea came to rule in Corinth by virtue of her descent from the Sun, bringing Jason with her. Here their children died. From one account it would seem that Medea, wishing to give them immortality, applied to them the same treatment she had pretended to give King Pelias. There was an accident, the children were killed, and Jason left her in disgust. This ironic turn of fortune would have made a tragedy in itself; but it is not the one that Euripides chose to write. According to another group of sources, the children were killed by the Corinthians, who afterwards spread the rumor that Medea had killed them herself.

3. THE PLAY

EURIPIDES, always more free in his adaptations of existing sources than either Aeschylus or Sophocles, makes several important changes, and his manipulation of the legend gives the clue to the purpose behind his play.

There are two striking differences. In the legend it is Medea who comes to rule in Corinth, with Jason only a secondary figure; and the motive for his desertion is his revulsion at the deaths of his children. In the play it is Jason who is well received in Corinth and Medea who is relegated to second place; and it is Jason who takes the initiative in deserting her, his motive being the purely selfish one of wishing to make a better match with the daughter of the royal house. Medea has no rights or hope of restitution; she is a foreign girl, a 'war bride' abandoned in a strange and hostile city.

Secondly, in the legend the children are killed accidentally, or by others; in the play Medea deliberately kills them herself. Euripides' originality in making these changes has been questioned, on somewhat doubtful grounds, but this need not concern us here. We must ask rather why he chose to use the version that he did, in preference to those more commonly accepted. The answer is that Euripides is attacking the slipshod morality implicit in the Golden Fleece story.

The voyage of the Argo seems at first sight to be a romantic tale of adventure, heroism and true love. The persecuted hero, sent on a mission which means almost certain death, wins the heart of a beautiful native girl; love laughs at dragons, and they sail away to live happily ever after. This is the very stuff of fairy tale; but, like so many fairy tales, it embodies incidents horrible in themselves of which we tend to lose sight beneath the romantic gloss which covers the whole. Here we have two such incidents, the deaths of Apsurtos and Pelias. It is Euripides' task to shake his audience out of their complacency and to demonstrate that stories they have accepted and enjoyed for years are in reality senseless and nauseating. In later plays he is to apply this technique to stories of gods, with more devastating consequences; here, although the subject-matter is slighter, he can still perform a salutary operation on the audience's conscience.

By placing more stress on Jason, and giving him the dominating position in Corinth, he prompts the audience to reconsider their romantic picture of their hero. Here Jason is shown as a self-seeking adventurer, sacrificing everything and everyone to his own career, and always ready to justify himself with specious arguments. What now of the Golden Fleece episode? If Jason behaves thus in Corinth, was there any real affection in his love-affair in Colchis? Or was he merely using Medea for his own advancement, as he is using the princess here?

The same treatment is applied to Medea herself. We watch her plotting the death of the princess; we hear that death, and the death of King Creon, described in one of the goriest speeches in all Greek tragedy; we hear the death-cries of her own children as she murders them. Four innocent people have died to further a personal revenge. Thus we are led to think again of the deaths of Apsurtos and Pelias. Do they seem so admirable now?

Early in the play Euripides inserts a deliberate hint of his intentions. In l. 234, Medea cries, "I have no mother, no brother, no family." Why has she no brother? Because she killed him. It is odd that this reference should come here, in an appeal to the chorus for sympathy, particularly since it does not occur where we might expect to find it, in Medea's self-defense before Jason. She lists all the things she has done for him (ll. 445 ff.) and we might reasonably expect her to add, "I even killed my brother for your sake." Its omission here makes the earlier reference stand out even more boldly. Euripides deliberately sacrifices probability to recall the death of Apsurtos to the audience's memory.

Even earlier in the play, Euripides has already made clear to us what we are to expect. The Nurse, in the middle of her conversation with the chorus, breaks off into a diatribe against "the old poets" who wrote for entertainment only (ll. 173 ff.). The function of the ancient poet was not merely to entertain but to teach. Drama in particular, with its unrivalled opportunities for reaching a large public, was expected to convey moral teaching, and lead the citizens in the way of truth and virtue. In the debate between the rival tragic poets which forms the second part of Aristophanes' *Frogs*, the questions discussed are more practical than literary: what can each poet do to help the state? Euripides voices through the Nurse his complaint that poetry in the past has taught nothing, but has merely encouraged the uncritical acceptance of such stories as he is attacking here, stories which every thinking man should reject.

Medea, then, shows popular mythology measured against moral and social standards and found wanting. Much of this must inevitably be lost on a modern audience. For a contemporary equivalent we must turn to plays such as *Les*

Chevaliers de la Table Ronde, Cocteau's cynical treatment of the Arthurian cycle. Cocteau stands in the same relation to Malory as Euripides to his legendary sources. But Euripides does much more than this. He brings the whole basis of morality into question by demonstrating how circumstances alter cases. Jason was only too happy to condone the crimes committed by Medea on his behalf; he is forced to revise his attitude when precisely similar crimes are committed against him. Jason comes to his own tragic realization at the end of the play (ll. 1269 ff.):

> Oh, now I know
> What I did not see before, it was a fatal curse
> To bring you from your foreign land to Greece,
> Traitor to your father and the land that reared you.
> The gods have turned your fury on my head.
> You killed your own brother there at your hearth-side
> Before you set foot on our good ship's deck,
> And this was your beginning.

In this respect the play is eternally relevant. Euripides shows how our estimate of the moral validity of an action depends on whether we benefit or suffer from it.

The play, then, is set against the legend; but there is another more subtle parallelism within the play itself. It falls into two parts, separated by the Aegeus scene, and the second balances, step by step, what has gone before. Jason deserts Medea, and she is condemned to exile, unable to return either to her own home or to that of her erstwhile husband. Euripides stresses her foreignness from the beginning, to make her isolation more complete. Aegeus' offer of refuge provides the turning point in her fortunes, and the diptychal structure of the play emphasizes the mathematical nature of Medea's revenge. Jason had deprived her of his love and her hopes of security. She deprives him of his new wife and his hopes for the future as represented by his sons. In the Greek world the continuance of the family line was all-important. Jason's attachment to his children is stressed throughout, and Medea's "You will not miss them yet; wait till you are older" is the bitterest taunt of all. He intended to leave her homeless while he lived in safety and prosperity. She now places him in exactly the same position. Neither Corinth nor Iolkos will be safe for him; but she may escape in the dragon chariot to find sanctuary in Athens. Their places have been completely reversed.

4. THE CHARACTERIZATION

THE characters of Medea and Jason have already been discussed above. It may be added that in his portrayal of Medea Euripides to some extent redeems himself from the charge of misogynism brought against him not only by his own generation but by later critics. Aristophanes, in the *Frogs*, makes Aeschylus accuse him of showing a succession of bad women in his plays; in another Aristophanic comedy, *Thesmophoriazousae*, the women of Athens are shown plotting vengeance on him for so often abusing their sex. It is true that in *Medea* the propensities of women to work harm are stressed; nevertheless Medea's magnificent opening speech on the hard lot of women in a man's world makes up for much.

In the character of Jason, Euripides finds time to hit out at another injustice, the Greek assumption of racial superiority and arrogance in dealing with other peoples. Greece was never a nation, but a collection of jealously independent cities united only by fear or force. There did, however, exist a consciousness of some common heritage which set the Greeks apart from the other peoples of the world. This was an attitude of mind to which the Athenians, boasting of the purity of their race, were particularly prone. Through Jason, Euripides administers a shrewd blow to this, one of the less amiable aspects of the Greek character. From the mouth of this self-seeking hypocrite comes a defense of the Greek virtues (ll. 504 ff.):

To start with, instead of living among savages
You live in Greece, and come to learn our laws
And how to live by justice, not brute force.

The audience is left to reflect what Greek justice has done for Medea. Euripides develops this theme more fully in other plays, particularly in the character of Odysseus in *Hecuba*. So far as *Medea* is concerned, the fact that Euripides could combine in one play this scathing criticism and a conventional patriotic ode is sufficient warning that we should be cautious in applying modern notions of consistency to the Greek dramatic experience.

Euripides was notorious in his own time for his attempts to bring the theatre down to earth, and to narrow the gap between drama and life. Aristophanes, again through the mouth of Aeschylus, censures his fondness for introducing characters from the lowest walks of life, not before deemed worthy of a place on the tragic stage. We see two of these in *Medea*, the Nurse and the Tutor—more accurately, a slave charged with the supervision of Jason's children—in whom Euripides brilliantly utilizes the gossip of the servants' hall to create atmosphere, and to arouse sympathy for Medea before she appears. The Tutor is a professed cynic, a man who can see through the pretensions of his masters; the Nurse is garrulous but kindly, genuinely fond of her mistress and the children, a simple soul caught up in events far above her head. In her we see a preliminary sketch for the far more formidable figure of Phaedra's old nurse in *Hippolytus*.

Creon and Aegeus to some extent counterbalance each other as two types of ruler. Creon, although he is responsible for sending Medea into exile, is not an unsympathetic figure. He is represented as a simple man whose one wish is to avoid trouble. In the end, it is his very kindness that is to prove his undoing, and his death is thereby all the more pathetic. Aegeus is a man in whom religious scruples are strong—a man of the old school who makes promises and keeps them—

though not without some tinge of self-interest. Where Creon acts on expediency, Aegeus recognizes deeper obligations, that old friends should be assisted and suppliants given protection. Thus Aegeus, epitomizing the old type of chivalry now fast vanishing, is contrasted not only with Creon but with Jason, the breaker of oaths.

5. THE PLAY AND ITS CRITICS

OF the objections raised against *Medea* by ancient and modern critics, three deserve to be considered in some detail.

a) *The Aegeus scene.* Critics from Aristotle onwards have objected that the appearance of Aegeus is too obviously contrived, to provide Medea with the refuge of which she has just spoken. If we are to assess the play in naturalistic terms, there is certainly some truth in this. But a naturalistic interpretation is the very thing we must beware of. Even in Euripides' hands, Greek tragedy is still a highly formal art, and a realistic representation of life is by no means the major consideration. The poet is concerned rather with form and structure, and the importance of this episode in the structure of the work has already been demonstrated. In addition, Aegeus' plight performs an important function in formulating Medea's final plan of revenge. Up to this point, she has thought only of killing her husband. The childlessness of Aegeus suggests the more terrible punishment of leaving Jason alive, but killing the children, and thereby depriving him of everything that makes life worth living.

Nor must we underestimate the interest of this scene for an Athenian audience. Here is an Athenian king arriving in the nick of time to rescue a heroine in distress. The Greek tragedians were never above playing on such patriotic feelings. Aegeus was an important figure in the legendary history of Athens and the father of Theseus, unifier of Attica, whom he was to beget soon after leaving Corinth. Thus the scene gives the audience a link with their own past.

Finally, the Aegeus scene prepares the way for the dragon chariot at the end. Aegeus emphasizes the difficulties of removing Medea from Corinth. Perhaps there is another inconsistency here. Euripides makes him speak almost as if he already foresaw the course Medea's actions would take. He insists, no less than three times (ll. 688 ff.), that he will not be responsible for taking her to Athens, but that she must make her own way there. Although Aegeus can know nothing of the plot—this is still a secret between Medea and the chorus—Euripides communicates to him something of her anxiety. The method of escape becomes all-important. It should be said that this inconsistency is not detrimental, but merely serves to give the scene a greater sense of urgency.

b) *The dragon chariot.* This has been condemned as a spectacular appendage, adding nothing to the play but serving merely to delight the eye. Euripides is certainly fond of such devices. He uses processions, stage spectacle and crowd scenes wherever there is opportunity. Audiences of the later fifth century were beginning to develop a taste for such displays, and the abandonment of the earlier simplicity and restraint for vivid and colorful effects becomes more and more apparent, not only in the theatre but in the visual arts generally. Euripides, a born showman, pandered to this taste, and *Medea* lends itself readily to such treatment. We may conjecture, from the evidence of vase paintings, that Euripides gave Medea an exotic oriental costume, and the dragon chariot in particular seems to have struck the audience's attention. Spectacle aside, however, it has already been argued that the chariot plays an essential part in the play's diptychal structure. To complete the perfect balance of the two halves, Medea must have a means of escape, and there is no illogicality in permitting her to call upon the resources of her witchcraft.

c) *The quarrel scene.* It has been objected that the confrontation of a faithless husband by his deserted wife, a scene calling for the wildest outpourings of passion, is here treated in too sophistical and artificial a spirit. Jason and Medea address each other in formal speeches, the first two of exactly equal length, and make points for the prosecution and defense more in the manner of a law-court than a domestic quarrel. But here again we must beware of applying modern standards to ancient tragedy. The Greek love of argument and debate, and, particularly in Athens, of litigation, permeates literature and the theatre, and does not confine itself to the courts and the council-house. It cannot be over-stressed that we are dealing here with formal drama, and that the set speeches, incongruous in the modern, naturalistic theatre, would have been accepted without comment by a Greek spectator. Nor must we forget the physical limitations by which the dramatist was bound. A modern playwright treating the same episode could allow many of Medea's reactions to go unspoken. The actress would signify her reception of Jason's defense by facial expression alone. This was denied to Euripides. Every point that Medea wishes to make, she must make verbally; and it is this that has led to the mistaken charges of artificiality and wordiness, by no means apparent in performance.

6. SUMMARY

Medea is a brilliant intellectual achievement, both as myth-criticism and an attack upon conventional morality. Although an early work, it demonstrates Euripides' technique at its most typical, and a masterly sense of construction. Its main weakness is one apparent throughout all Euripides' work, the handling of the chorus. At this stage in the history of the Greek theatre, the chorus has lost its old importance. Euripides, attempting to create a new type of realistic tragedy within the old conventional framework, finds it more and more of an embarrassment, particularly in plays of intrigue such as this, where the constant presence of the chorus makes it necessary for Medea, unnaturally, to confide in them. Nevertheless, the songs on the infidelity of man and in praise of Athens are two of his major choral compositions, worthy of a place beside those of Sophocles.

Medea, however, owes its survival more to its theatrical than to its purely intellectual qualities. The plays of Euripides, too unorthodox to be popular in his lifetime, were eagerly revived after his death, when the controversy that initially surrounded them was forgotten, and were performed far more frequently than those of Aeschylus or Sophocles. For Euripides is a master of the art of the theatre; his power to create exciting scenes and powerful characters has kept him popular with actors and audiences alike. In our own time, leading actresses—Katina Paxinou, Judith Anderson, Eileen Herlie, Sybil Thorndike—have found in the character of Medea a fit vehicle for their own talents. *Medea* ranks not far below *Oedipus Rex* as one of the most popular Greek Plays in the modern repertory.

ACKNOWLEDGMENTS

In preparing this analysis of *Medea*, I have been assisted substantially by the copious commentary in Professor Denys Page's edition of the play (Oxford, Clarendon Press, 1952) and also by Professor T. E. Buttrey's article, "Accident and Design in Euripides' *Medea*" (*American Journal of Philology*, LXXIX, 1958), which throws an important new light on the formal structure of the work. I must also record my gratitude to my friend and sometime tutor, Mr. A. D. Fitton-Brown of the University College of North Wales, for numerous valuable suggestions embodied here.

CHARACTERS

NURSE to Medea
TUTOR to Medea's children
The two sons of Medea and Jason
CHORUS of Corinthian women
MEDEA
CREON, King of Corinth
JASON
AEGEUS, King of Athens
MESSENGER
Soldiers, servants and attendants.

The action takes place before the house of MEDEA *in Corinth.*
MEDEA'S *old* NURSE *is standing at the door.*

NURSE
If only Argo's hull had never flown
Between the Clashing Rocks to Colchis' shore,
And if the pine in Pelion's woods had never
Been chopped down, to put oars into the hands
Of heroes who went out in Pelias' name
To fetch the Golden Fleece! My mistress then,
Medea, would never have fallen in love with Jason
And sailed with him to the walls of Iolkos' land,
Or persuaded the daughters of Pelias to kill
Their father; would not be living here   10
In Corinth, with her husband and her children,
Giving pleasure to the country she has chosen for her exile.
Everything she did was for Jason's sake,
And that's the best way of avoiding risks,
For a wife to have no quarrel with her husband.
But love's turned sour, there's hatred everywhere.
Jason deserts my mistress and his children
And seeks a royal alliance, marrying
The daughter of Creon, ruler of this land,
While poor Medea is left wretched and dishonored   20
To cry "You promised," and remind him of the hand
He pledged in faith, and calls on heaven to see
What she has done for him—and her reward.
She lies without eating, her body abandoned to grief,
Weeping herself thinner with each day that passed
Since first she knew her husband was unfaithful,
Never lifting her head or raising her eyes
From the ground, as deaf as rock or water
To anyone who gives her good advice.
Except, at times, she lifts her snow-white neck   30
And mourns to herself for the loss of her dear father
And the home and country she betrayed to come

27

Away with a man who now cares nothing for her.
Poor lady, she has come to learn the hard way
What it means to have no country to go back to.
She hates her children, takes no joy in seeing them;
I'm afraid she has something dreadful in her mind.
She's a dangerous woman; he who picks a fight
With her won't come off victor easily.
Here come her children, leaving their games behind;   40
They don't know anything about their mother's
Sorrows; youth is no friend to grief.

(*Enter* MEDEA's *two small sons, with their* TUTOR.)

TUTOR
My mistress' time-worn piece of household property,
What are you doing standing here alone
Before the gates, soliloquizing on misfortune?
However could Medea do without you?

NURSE
Old fellow, guardian of Jason's children,
Good servants take it as a personal sorrow
When trouble and misfortune touch their masters.
And I was moved to such a pitch of misery   50
I longed to come outside, to tell
Heaven and earth about Medea's troubles.

TUTOR
Poor lady, has she not stopped weeping yet?

NURSE
O blessed ignorance! Not halfway, hardly started.

TUTOR
The fool—if I may speak so of my mistress;
She knows nothing of her more recent troubles.

NURSE
What is it, old man? Don't keep it to yourself!

TUTOR
Nothing. I'm sorry that I said so much.

NURSE

By your beard, don't keep it from your fellow-servant.
I'll swear to keep it secret if I must.   60

TUTOR

I heard somebody saying, and pretended not to listen,
When I was at the place where the old men sit
Playing draughts around the holy fountain of Peirene,
That Creon, this country's ruler, was about
To send Medea with her children into exile
Away from Corinth. Whether this tale is true
I cannot say; I hope it may not be so.

NURSE

Will Jason be content to see his sons
So treated, even though he's quarrelled with their mother?

TUTOR

When loyalties conflict, the old one loses.   70
He has no love for any in this house.

NURSE

Why then, we are ruined, if we must add new sorrow
Before we have got rid of the old one.

TUTOR

This is no time to tell Medea
What has happened; be quiet, keep it to yourself.

NURSE

My children, do you see what your father's like?
I hope he—no, he is my master still,
Even though he's proved a traitor to his loved ones.

TUTOR

Who isn't? Have you only just now realized
That no man puts his neighbor before himself?   80
Some have good reason, most are out for profit,
Just as he neglects his sons for his new wife's sake.

NURSE

Go indoors, my children, everything will be all right.

You keep them to themselves as much as possible,
Don't bring them near their mother when she's angry.
I saw that wild bull look come in her eyes
As if she meant them harm. I know too well
She'll keep her anger warm till someone's hurt.
May it be enemies, and not her friends!

(MEDEA's *voice is heard from inside the house.*)

MEDEA

Oh,
I am wretched and oppressed with troubles.   90
I wish I were dead, I wish I were dead.

NURSE

What did I tell you, dear children? Your mother
Is stirring her heart and her anger with it.
Get along indoors as quickly as possible,
Don't go within sight of her, don't come near her,
Beware of her temper, the wild beast lurking
In that desperate mind of hers.
Come now, hurry along indoors;
It's clear that her smoldering anger will burst
Into flames as her passion increases.   100
Her spirit's too big for her, uncontrollable;
What will she do when provoked?

MEDEA

Oh,
I have suffered things, I have suffered things
Worth a world of weeping. Unhappy sons,
May you die with your father, the whole house perish!

NURSE

Oh dear, oh dear, what a state I am in!
What have your children to do with their father's
Wickedness, why hate them?
Oh, my darling children,
I'm terrified something will happen to you.   110

It's bad when a queen is angry; she rarely submits,
Gets her own way in most things, and changes
Her mood without warning.

(*Exeunt* CHILDREN *and* TUTOR.)

It's better if you've been used to a life
Without any ups or downs; I'd rather
Grow old in peace than be a great lady.
Moderation's a word that's good to hear
And the greatest blessing that men could have.
Excess can never bring profit; when heaven's
Angry, the great ones are hit the hardest.   120

(*Enter the* CHORUS *of Corinthian women.*)

CHORUS
I heard the voice, I heard the cry
Of Colchis' unhappy daughter.
It is ringing still; tell us, old woman.
I was inside at my door, and heard her crying.
I cannot be happy when the home is troubled,
When the home is one I love.

NURSE
Home! There is no home, that's past and gone.
Jason is wrapped up in his new wife,
And my mistress sits pining away in her room
And her friends can say nothing to comfort her.   130

MEDEA
I wish
That lightning from heaven would split my head open!
What have I to live for now?
Why can I not leave this hateful life
And find repose in death?

CHORUS
Zeus, heaven and earth, do you hear
How the wretched wife is weeping?

Why do you pray for that hateful sleep?
Fool, would you wish your death sooner?
This is no way to pray. If your husband   140
Honors another wife, it has happened
To others, don't take it to heart.
Zeus will see justice done; don't wear
Yourself out with lamenting your husband.

MEDEA

Goddess of justice, Queen Artemis,
You see how I suffer, who bound
My husband, curse him, with oaths?
I pray I may see him perish
And his wife, and all the house
Who have dared unprovoked to wrong me.   150
My father, my country, how shamefully
I left you, and killed my own brother.

NURSE

Do you hear what she says, how she cries
To Themis in prayer, and to Zeus
Whom we honor as keeper of oaths?
One thing is certain, my mistress
Won't let go her anger for nothing.

CHORUS

If she would only come out here to see us,
If she would only hear what we have to say,
To see if her bitterness would melt   160
And her anger disappear.
I hope I shall always be ready
To stand by my friends. Go inside, old woman,
And fetch her out of the house; and hurry,
Before she can harm the household;
That's the way her grief is going.

NURSE

I'll do it, but I'm afraid
I shan't be able to move her.

Still, it's a labor of love.
She's angry, and glares at her servants   170
Like a lioness guarding her cubs
When anyone comes with a message.
You wouldn't be wrong to consider
The old poets not clever but fools
Who wrote music for dinners and banquets,
Pleasant tunes for men who were happy,
But nobody ever discovered
How to use all this music and singing
To lessen a man's load of trouble
That brought death and misfortune and ruin.   180
It would certainly be an advantage
To use music for healing! Why waste it
On dinners? There's pleasure enough
In a banquet, who wants any more?

(*Exit.*)

CHORUS

I heard the voice heavy with grief
Bitterly mourning the faithless
Husband who married and left her,
Blaming her wrongs on the gods,
The justice of Zeus, the sworn oath
That started her difficult crossing   190
Through the gates of the salt foggy sea
To the opposite shores of Greece.

(*Enter* MEDEA.)

MEDEA

Women of Corinth, I have come outside
To avoid your disapproval. I know there are many
Conceited people; some keep themselves to themselves,
Others show it in public, while others still, who take
Things quietly, will find themselves called idlers.
The eyes are no good judges, when a man
Dislikes another at sight before he knows

His character, when there is nothing against him. 200
A foreigner especially should conform.
I'd even blame a native for presuming
To annoy his fellow citizens through lack of manners.
For me, this unexpected blow that fell
Has shattered me; it is the end, I only want to die.
The man to whom I gave my all, as well he knows,
Has turned out utterly false—my husband.
Of all things living that possess a mind
We women are the most unfortunate.
To start with, we must put ourselves to vast expense 210
To buy ourselves a husband, take a master for
Our bodies—a worse evil than the other:
And everything depends on this, whether we take a good man
Or a bad one; divorce is not respectable
For women, we may not deny our husbands.
Coming to new manners and a new way of life,
A woman needs second sight to know how best
To manage her bedfellow; no-one taught her at home.
And if we work hard at it, and our husband
Lives with us without struggling against the yoke 220
We are to be envied; if not, death comes at last.
When a man is bored with the company in his household
He can go out to find his consolation.
We women have only one soul-mate to look to.
They tell us we can spend our lives at home
In safety, while they go out to fight the wars.
How illogical! I'd rather stand three times
In the battlefield than bear one child.
But we have different stories, you and I;
You have a city, and a father's home, 230
And friendly company, a life you can enjoy.
I have no home, no country; I am despised
By my husband, something brought back from abroad;
I have no mother, no brother, no family
Where I can find a refuge from my troubles.

So this is the favor I will ask of you:
If the means offer, or I can find some way
To pay my husband back for the wrong he has done me,
Keep my secret. At other times a woman is timid,
Afraid to defend herself, frightened at the sight   240
Of weapons; but when her marriage is in danger
There is no mind bloodthirstier than hers.

CHORUS

I will; for you have every right to punish him.
I do not wonder that you are distressed.
But I can see Creon, ruler of this land,
Approaching with some new decision to tell us.

(*Enter* CREON.)

CREON

You with the scowling face, who hate your husband,
Medea, I command you leave this land
An exile, taking your two children with you
Without delay. I come to execute   250
My own decree, and shall not go back home
Till I have seen you past our boundaries.

MEDEA

Alas, my ruin is complete;
My enemies pursue full-sailed, and I
Can find no friendly harbor from calamity.
But though I am persecuted I will ask one thing:
For what reason, Creon, do you banish me?

CREON

I am afraid of you. Why veil my words?
Afraid you will do my child some dreadful harm.
And many things contribute to my fear: 260
You are clever, and accomplished in black arts,
And angry that your husband has deserted you.
I hear you threaten—so I am informed—
To act against the bridegroom and the bride

And the father too. I had rather be safe than sorry.
Better be hated, woman, by you now,
Than soften and repent my weakness later.

MEDEA
This has happened before. It is not the first time, Creon,
I have been the victim of my reputation.
No sensible man should ever have his sons   270
Brought up more clever than the average.
Apart from being told they waste their time
They earn the spite and envy of their neighbors.
You'll be called good-for-nothing, not intelligent,
For holding unconventional ideas;
And if the know-alls find your reputation
Exceeding theirs, the state will turn against you.
And I am one of those to whom it happened.
I am clever, so some people envy me,
Some call me idle, some the opposite,   280
While others hate me; but they exaggerate.
You fear me? Do you think you will be hurt?
I am in no state—do not be nervous, Creon—
To commit an offence against the authorities.
How have you wronged me? You bestowed your daughter
On the man your heart desired. It is my husband
That I hate.
But I suppose you know what you are doing.
I do not grudge you any of your good fortune.
Let the marriage stand, and prosper; but permit me   290
To stay here. Though I am the injured party
I shall not raise my voice against my betters.

CREON
Your words are smooth enough, but I fear your heart
Is already plotting mischief, and by so much less
I trust you than I did before.
A fiery temper, in woman as in man,
Is easier to guard against than silent cunning.

So get you gone without more argument.
You may be sure that no arts you can use
Will keep you here, now you have turned against us.   300

MEDEA
No, by your knees, and by your child the bride!

CREON
Go, it is useless, you cannot persuade me.

MEDEA
Will you turn me away and not listen to my prayers?

CREON
My family comes first in my affections.

MEDEA
My country, how strongly I recall you now.

CREON
I love my country too, after my children.

MEDEA
Oh, what a bitter curse is love to men.

CREON
Well, that depends on circumstances, I suppose.

MEDEA
O Zeus, remember who began these sorrows.

CREON
Get out, you fool, and trouble me no further.   310

MEDEA
I have my troubles; trouble me no further.

CREON
Soon my men will drive you out by force.

MEDEA
No! Spare me that, at least. I beg you, Creon—

CREON
You seem determined, woman, to be difficult.

MEDEA

No. I will go. It was not that I wanted.

CREON

Then why resist? Why do you not leave the country?

MEDEA

Permit me to remain here this one day,
To make my mind up where I am to go,
And where to keep my children, since their father
Prefers to leave his sons without protection.   320
You are a father; you have sons yourself,
And therefore should be well disposed to mine.
I do not care for myself if I am banished
But I am wretched if they are in trouble.

CREON

I never had the heart to play the tyrant.
My conscience has always been my disadvantage.
Woman, I know that I am making a mistake,
But your request is granted. But I warn you,
If the light of heaven falls on you tomorrow
Here with your sons inside our boundaries   330
You die. This is my final word.
And now, if stay you must, remain one day,
Too little time to do the harm I dread.

(*Exit.*)

CHORUS

How troubled you are, unfortunate lady!
Where will you turn? What home, what country
Will give you protection?
Medea, god has plunged you in a sea of troubles
And there is no land in sight.

MEDEA

Beaten on every side; who can deny it?
But not in this, so do not think I am.   340
There are still trials for this new-married pair

And no small sorrow for their families.
You think I would have fawned upon this man
Unless I were working for my own advantage?
I would not have touched him, not have spoken to him.
But he has gone so far in foolishness
That when he could have foiled my plans
By sending me to exile, he allowed me stay
One day, in which I shall make corpses of
Three of my enemies—father, girl, my husband.   350
And I have many ways to work their deaths
And do not know where first to try my hand—
Whether to set their wedding house on fire,
Or creep indoors to where their bedroom is
And thrust a sharpened sword into their hearts.
One thing prevents me; if I should be caught
Entering the house and plotting against it
I shall die the laughing-stock of my enemies.
No. It is best to go direct, the way in which I am
Most skilled, and poison both of them.   360
Ah then,
Suppose them dead; what city will receive me?
What host will offer me home and security
In some safe country, and protect my life?
No-one. Then I shall wait a little while,
And if some tower of safety should appear,
By stealth and cunning I shall murder them.
But if misfortune should drive me out helpless,
I shall take the sword, even though it means my death,
And kill them.
No, by the Queen of Night whom above all   370
I honor and have chosen as my partner,
Dark Hecate dwelling in the corners of my hearth,
No man shall wound my heart and still live happy.
I will make them curse the day they married,
Curse this alliance and my banishment.
Then come, Medea, call on all the skill

You have in plotting and contriving;
On to the crime! This is the test of courage.
Look to your wrongs! You must not let yourself
Be mocked by Jason's Sisyphean wedding,   380
You, a royal child, descended from the Sun.
You have the skill; moreover you were born
A woman; and women are incapable of good,
But have no equal in contriving harm.

CHORUS

The sacred rivers flow back to their sources,
The appointed order of things is reversed.
It is men whose minds are deceitful, who take
The names of their gods in vain,
And women the future will honor in story
As leaders of upright lives.   390
Glory is ours! And the slanderous tongues
That attacked womankind shall be stilled.

You Muses of past generations, inspire
No more the refrain that woman is fickle.
We were not given the wit by Phoebus
Apollo, the master of songs,
To strike from the lyre its heavenly music.
If it were so, I should sing
In answer to men; for history tells
As much of men's lives as of ours.   400

In passion you sailed from the land
Of your fathers, and saw the twin rocks
Of the sea fall open before you.
Now you live among strangers, exchange
Your couch for a husbandless bed;
Without rights and distressed you are driven
An exile out of the land.

The spell of the oath has been broken; no longer
Has Greece any shame, it has flown to the winds.
Poor lady, your father's home   410

Will offer you shelter no more
In time of distress; your marriage
Is lost to a queen who descends
On your house as a second bride.

(*Enter* JASON.)

JASON

I have noticed many times, this not the first,
How willfulness runs on to self-destruction.
You could have kept this country as your home
By obeying the decisions of your betters,
But futile protests send you into exile.
They do not worry me. You can go on   420
Forever saying Jason is a scoundrel;
But when it comes to slandering your rulers,
Count yourself lucky you were only banished.
I wanted you to stay—tried all the time
To pacify the anger of the king;
But you persevered in folly, and continually
Spoke ill of him, and so you must be banished.
However, I shall not desert my friends
In spite of their behavior, but am here to see
That you and your children do not go out penniless   430
Or in need of anything; for banishment
Brings many hardships. Hate me though you may,
I could never bring myself to bear you malice.

MEDEA

Oh, devil! Devil! This is the worst abuse
My tongue can find for your lack of manliness.
You come to me, my mortal enemy,
Hateful to heaven and to all mankind?
This is not venturesome, this is not courage,
To look friends in the face whom you have wronged,
But the most detestable of human weaknesses,   440
Yes, shamelessness! But I am glad you came,
For I can ease my overburdened heart

Abusing you, and you will smart to hear.
I shall begin my tale at the beginning.
I saved your life, as every single Greek
Who sailed with you on board the Argo knows,
When you were sent to tame the bulls that breathed fire,
And yoke them, and sow death in the field.
The dragon that encircled with his coils
The Golden Fleece and watched it without sleeping   450
I killed for you, and lit your path to safety.
For you I left my father and my home
And sailed to Iolkos and Mount Pelion
With you, and showed more eagerness then sense.
I brought on Pelias the worst of ends,
Death at his children's hands, and ruined his house.
All this I suffered for your worthless sake,
To be abandoned for another woman,
Though I had borne you children! Were I barren
You might have some excuse to marry again.   460
I have no faith in your promises; I cannot tell
If you believe in the old gods still, or think
There is some newer standard of morality—
You have broken your oath to me, you must know that.
Oh, this my right hand, that you wrung so often!
These knees, at which you fell; how am I deceived
In a false lover, cheated of my hopes.
But come, I will open my heart to you as to a friend—
Though what fair treatment could I hope from you?
Yet will I; you will feel more shame to answer.   470
Where should I turn now? To my father's home?
The country I betrayed to come with you?
Or Pelias' wretched daughters? They would give
A gracious welcome to their father's murderess.
For that is how it is. I have estranged myself
From friends at home, and those I should not hurt
I have made mortal enemies for your sake.
In recompense, how happy have you made me

Among Greek women; what a paragon
Of rectitude I married, to my sorrow,   480
When I am exiled, cast out of the land
Without a friend. My sons are all I have.
A fine reproach for this new-married man
When his sons and she who saved him wander beggars.
O Zeus, why have you given men clear marks
To help them tell true gold from counterfeit,
While nature sets no stamp upon men's bodies
To help us tell the true man from the false!

CHORUS
Tempers run high, and cannot soon be soothed,
When those who have once loved begin to quarrel.   490

JASON
I must show myself no mean speaker, so it seems,
But like the sea-wise steersman of a ship
Close-haul my canvas, lady, and run before
The storm of your verbosity. Since you
Have raised this monument to your own kindness,
I hold that Cypris was the guardian of my voyages,
No other god or man. You are quick-witted, true,
But it would be ungenerous to explain
You were compelled by Love's unerring shafts to save me.
However, I shall not go too deeply into that;   500
Where you did help me, you did not do badly.
But you have profited by my escape
More than you lost by it. Let me explain:
To start with, instead of living among savages
You live in Greece and come to learn our laws
And how to live by justice, not brute force.
Besides, all Greece has learned how clever you are.
You're famous! If you still lived at the ends
Of the earth, nobody would have heard of you.
If only my good fortune made me famous,   510
I would not ask for riches, nor the power

To sing a sweeter song than Orpheus did.
So much for what you have to say about
My labors; you began the argument.
For your reproaches on my royal marriage,
I'll show you first of all how clever I was,
Second, how prudent, and third, that I am my sons'
And your best friend. Please do not interrupt me.
When, with this irretrievable misfortune
Behind me, I came here from Iolkos' land,   520
What better piece of luck could I have found
Than this, an exile marry a princess?
Not that you bored me—the sore point with you—
Or that I was infatuated with a new wife
Or anxious for a larger family;
I'm satisfied with those I already have.
No! My main reason was that we should live well,
Not have to count our pennies. I'm aware
How all friends turn against you when you're poor.
I wanted to bring my children up as sons of mine   530
Should be, and give my sons by you some brothers.
If I could join our families and make them one,
I'd count myself a happy man. You need no sons,
But it profits me to add to those I have. Is this
So reprehensible? It's only jealousy
That makes you think so. But things have come to such a pass
That women think marriage is the only thing that matters.
When once your sole possession is endangered,
Whatever's good and right for you to do
You fight it. There ought to be some other way   540
For men to get their sons, there ought to be
No women; then a man could live his life in peace.

CHORUS
Jason, you have made a pretty speech,
But I will be bold, and say what I think:
It was criminal to desert your wife.

MEDEA

The world and I have very different views.
The bad man who is clever with his tongue
In my opinion asks for double punishment.
He prides himself on his power to talk his way
Out of everything, nothing frightens him. But he   550
Is not so clever as he thinks. So do not make
Fine speeches, or think to play the innocent
With me. One word will throw you. If you were honest
You should have told me of your wedding plans,
Not kept them secret from the ones that loved you.

JASON

Much good you would have done my wedding plans, I must say,
If I'd told you of them, when even now
You can't disguise the anger in your heart.

MEDEA

It was not that. You thought it might cause talk
To have a foreign wife when you grew older.   560

JASON

I tell you it was not for the woman's sake
I made the royal alliance that I did,
But as I said before, to offer you
Protection, and beget young kings to be
My sons' new brothers, towers of strength to us.

MEDEA

Give me no happiness involving pain
Or joy that will not leave the mind in peace.

JASON

You should know better; pray for something else,
Never to judge good fortune to be bad
Or count yourself hard done by when all's well.   570

MEDEA

Go on, insult me! You have a place to go
While I am an exile from the land and friendless.

JASON

You brought it on yourself, blame no-one else.

MEDEA

How? Did I marry and abandon you?

JASON

Calling down blasphemous curses on the king.

MEDEA

Yes, you will find me a curse to your house too.

JASON

I refuse to discuss this matter any further.
But if you want my money, to assist
You and your children when you are gone,
Speak out; I am ready to be open-handed,   580
And give you introductions to my friends
Who will assist you. It is foolish to refuse;
Let your anger rest, and you will profit by it.

MEDEA

I want no truck with any friends of yours
Or anything from you, so do not offer it.
A bad man's gifts bring no-one any good.

JASON

Very well! But I call on heaven to witness
I have done everything possible for you and your sons.
Your stubbornness rejects your friends; you don't know
When you are well off. So much the worse for you.   590

(*Exit.*)

MEDEA

Yes, go; you are too eager for your new bride
To stay any longer outside her house.
Go and be married! God will echo me,
This marriage may be such you will disown it.

CHORUS

Love unrestrained can bring

No worth or honor with it,
But coming in small measure
There is no power more gracious.
Never let fly at me
Great Queen, the unerring shafts   600
Of your golden arrows, tipped
In the poison of desire.

Let moderation be
My guide, the gods' best gift.
Dread Aphrodite, never
Send strife and argument
To attack my heart and make
Me long for other loves,
But learn to honor marriage
And let love lie in peace.   610

Oh, let me never lose you,
My country and my home,
Or learn the thorny ways
Of poverty, the worst
Of life's calamities.
No! Let me rather die
And see life's brief day done.
This is the greatest sorrow,
The loss of fatherland.

I know; I do not learn   620
The tale from the lips of others.
No home or friend to share
The depths of your distress.
Dishonored be the man
Who honors not his friends
And locks his heart away;
No friend shall he be of mine.

(*Enter* AEGEUS.)

AEGEUS
Give you joy, Medea; this is the best way

Men know to start a conversation with their friends.

MEDEA
And joy to you, wise Aegeus, son of Pandion.   630
Where are you from? What brings you to our country?

AEGEUS
From Apollo's ancient oracle at Delphi.

MEDEA
What took you there, to earth's prophetic center?

AEGEUS
To inquire how children might be born to me.

MEDEA
What, are you still without a son at your age?

AEGEUS
Yes, by some whim of providence I have no heir.

MEDEA
Are you married? Or have you never had a wife?

AEGEUS
I am no stranger to the marriage bond.

MEDEA
And what did Phoebus have to say about it?

AEGEUS
Words too wise for a man to understand.   640

MEDEA
Then may I know the oracle's reply?

AEGEUS
Most certainly, for cleverness is what we need.

MEDEA
Then tell me, if you may, what Phoebus said.

AEGEUS
Not to loosen the wineskin's hanging foot—

MEDEA
Until you had arrived somewhere, or done something?

AEGEUS
Until I reached my ancestral hearth again.

MEDEA
And what directs your journey through this country?

AEGEUS
There is a man called Pittheus, King of Troezen—

MEDEA
Old Pelops' son, with a great reputation for piety.

AEGEUS
I want to tell him what the oracle has said.   650

MEDEA
He is a wise man, skillful in such matters.

AEGEUS
And the oldest of my military allies.

MEDEA
I hope you are lucky, and achieve your heart's desire.

(*She breaks down, and turns away her head.*)

AEGEUS
Why do you turn away, and look so pale?

MEDEA
Aegeus, my husband is the worst of men.

AEGEUS
What's this you say? Tell me about your troubles.

MEDEA
Jason, unprovoked, has done me wrong.

AEGEUS
What has he done to you? Tell me more clearly.

MEDEA
Put another woman over his household in my place.

AEGEUS
He would not dare to treat you so despicably!   660

MEDEA
Too truly; and I, the old love, am dishonored.

AEGEUS
Was it for love of her, or hate of you?

MEDEA
Much love he has; the man was born unfaithful.

AEGEUS
Take no notice, if he's as worthless as you say.

MEDEA
He was in love with marrying a king's daughter.

AEGEUS
Who gives her to him? Tell me the whole story.

MEDEA
Creon, the ruler of this land of Corinth.

AEGEUS
You have good reason for your grief, my lady.

MEDEA
It is the end; and I am banished too.

AEGEUS
On whose orders? This is a new wrong you speak of.   670

MEDEA
It is Creon who sends me into exile from the land.

AEGEUS
And Jason lets him? This is unforgivable.

MEDEA
He says not, but he has resigned himself.

(*She falls at his feet.*)

But I beseech you, by the beard I clasp,
And throw myself a suppliant at your knees,
Have pity, have pity on my misery
And do not see me thrown out destitute.

Let me come to your country and live at your hearthside;
So may your great desire come to fruition
And give you children, and allow you to die happy. 680
You do not know what good fortune you have found.
I can put a stop to your childlessness, and give
You issue, with the potions that I know.

AEGEUS

I am anxious for many reasons, lady,
To grant your request; first, my religious scruples,
And then your promise that I should have sons,
For in this there is nothing else that I can do.
But this is how I stand. If you can reach my country
I'll endeavor to protect you as in duty bound.
But one thing I must make clear from the start: 690
I am not willing to take you from this country.
If you can make your own way to my home
I will keep you safe and give you up to no-one,
But you must make your own escape from Corinth.
I would not give offence, even to strangers.

MEDEA

So let it be, then. If you swear an oath
To do this, I have nothing more to ask.

AEGEUS

Do you not trust me? What is it puts you off?

MEDEA

I trust you; but the house of Pelias is against me,
And Creon. Oath-bound, you could never yield 700
Me to them when they came to take me away.
A promise unsupported by an oath
Would allow you to befriend them, and obey
Their summons when it came. My cause is weak,
While they have power and money on their side.

AEGEUS

You show great thought for the future in what you say.

But, if you wish it, I shall not refuse.
My own position will be unassailable
If I have an excuse to offer your enemies,
And you will run less risk. Come, name your gods.   710

MEDEA
Swear by the plain of Earth, and by the Sun,
My father's father; add the whole family of gods.

AEGEUS
That I will do or not do what? Say on.

MEDEA
Never to drive me from the land yourself
Or willingly yield me to my enemies
When they come for me, as long as you do live.

AEGEUS
I swear by Earth, by the holy light of Sun,
By all the gods, to do as you have said.

MEDEA
Enough. What penalty if you break your oath?

AEGEUS
What comes to men who take their gods in vain.   720

MEDEA
Now go your way in peace. All will be well.
I shall come to your country as soon as I have done
What I intend to do, and won my heart's desire.

CHORUS
Now Hermes, God of Travelers,
Give you safe conduct home,
And may the desire that you cherish
So eagerly be fulfilled.
You have shown, Aegeus,
What a good man you are.

(*Exit* AEGEUS.)

MEDEA
O Zeus, Zeus' daughter Justice, light of Sun,   730

Now shall we have a glorious triumph, friends,
Upon our enemies; our feet are on the path.
Now is there hope my enemies will pay
The penalty. This man has shown himself,
Where we were weakest, a haven for my plans.
In him my ship may find safe anchorage;
To Athena's fortress city shall I go!
And now I will reveal you all my plans.
Hear what I have to say; it will not please you.
One of my servants I shall send to Jason   740
And ask him to come here before my face.
And when he comes, I shall say soft words to him,
That I agree with him, and all is well;
That the royal match he abandons me to make
Is for my advantage, and a good idea.
I shall entreat him that my sons should stay—
Not to allow my sons to be insulted
In a strange country by my enemies,
But to kill the daughter of the king with cunning.
I shall send them both with presents in their hands,   750
A fine-spun robe, a golden diadem.
If she accepts the gifts and puts them on
She will die in agony and all who touch her,
With such deadly poison shall I anoint my gifts.
Now I must leave this story, and lament
The dreadful thing that then remains for me to do.
I will kill my sons; no man shall take them from me.
And when the house of Jason lies in ruins,
I shall fly this land, setting my darlings' death
Behind me, most unspeakable of crimes.   760
The scorn of enemies is unendurable.
But let it go; for what have I to live for?
I have no home, no country, no escape from misery.
I made my mistake the day I left behind
My father's home, seduced by speeches from
A Greek who heaven knows will pay for them.
The sons I bore him he will never see

Alive after this day, nor father more
On his new-married bride, condemned to die
In agony from my poisons as she deserves.   770
No-one shall call me timorous or weak
Or stay-at-home, but quite the opposite,
A menace to my enemies and help to friends;
Those are the people that the world remembers.

CHORUS

Since you have taken me into your confidence,
I should like to help you, but must still uphold
The laws of men. I say you cannot do this.

MEDEA

There is nothing else I can do. But you have excuse
For speaking so, you have not known my sufferings.

CHORUS

But will you have the heart to kill your children?   780

MEDEA

Yes; it is the way I can most hurt my husband.

CHORUS

But you will be the most unhappy of women.

MEDEA

So be it; there can be no compromise.

(*Calling the* NURSE.)

You; go at once and fetch Jason here.
We have no secrets from each other, you and I.
And breathe no word to anyone of my plans,
As you love your mistress, as you are a woman.

(*Exit* NURSE.)

CHORUS

Happy of old were the sons of Erechtheus,
Sprung from the blessed gods, and dwelling
In Athens' holy and untroubled land.   790

Their food is glorious wisdom; they walk
With springing step in the crystal air.
Here, so they say, golden Harmony first
Saw the light, the child of the Muses nine.

And here too, they say, Aphrodite drank
Of Cephisus' fair-flowing stream, and breathed
Sweet breezes over the land, with garlands
Of scented roses entwined in her hair,
And gave Love a seat on the throne of Wisdom
To work all manner of arts together.   800

How then will this city of sacred waters,
This guide and protector of friends, take you,
Your children's slayer, whose touch will pollute
All others you meet? Think again of the deaths
Of your children, the blood you intend to shed.
By your knees, by every entreaty we beg you
Not to become your children's murderess.

Where will you find the boldness of mind,
The courage of hand and heart, to kill them?
How will you strike without weeping, how   810
Be constant to stain your hands in their blood
When your children kneel weeping before you?

(*Enter* JASON.)

JASON

I come at your request; although you hate me,
This favor you shall have. So let me hear
What new demand you have to make of me.

MEDEA

Jason, I ask you to forgive the words
I spoke just now. The memory of our
Past love should help you bear my evil temper.
Now I have taken myself to task and found
I was to blame. "Fool, why am I so mad?   820

Why should I quarrel with those who want to help me,
And why antagonize the men in power
And my husband, who works only for my advantage
In making this royal marriage, and begetting
New brothers for my sons? Why not lay down
My anger, why resent what the gods provide?
Are not the children mine, and am I not
An exile from the land, without a friend?"
Such were my thoughts; and then I realized
What foolishness my futile anger was.   830
Now I agree with you, and think you provident
In gaining us this connection, and myself a fool.
I should have been your go-between and shared
Your plans, stood by your marriage-bed,
And had the joy of tending your new bride.
But we are what we are; I will not say bad,
But women. But you should not take bad example
And answer my stupidity with yours.
Now I submit, agree that I was wrong
Before, but come to saner judgment now.   840
My children, here, my children, leave the house,
Come out to greet your father, and with me
Bid him goodbye; be reconciled to friends
And let your anger rest beside your mother's.

(*The* CHILDREN *appear from the house, and go to* JASON.)

We are at peace; there is no anger now.
Come, take his hand.
(*aside*)   Oh, the pity of it;
There is something still unseen, but my mind knows it.
Children, will you live long to stretch out
Your loving arms, as now? Oh pity, pity;
How near I am to tears, how full of fear.   850
(*aloud*)
At last I have stopped the quarrel with their father
And brought tears of forgiveness to their eyes.

CHORUS

And my eyes too are wet with running tears.
I pray we have no troubles worse than these.

JASON

I approve this mood, and do not blame the other.
It is natural for a woman to show resentment
When her husband smuggles in a second marriage.
But now your mind has turned to better things
And learned—at last—which policy must win.
Done like a sensible woman!   860

(*To the* CHILDREN.)

Your father hasn't forgotten you, my boys.
God willing, you'll be well provided for.
I'll see you here in Corinth at the top
Beside your brothers. Just grow up; your father
Will see to the rest, and any god that fancies you.
I want to see you, when you've grown young men,
Stout fellows, head and shoulders above my enemies.
Medea, what are these tears upon your cheeks?
Why do you turn your face away from me?
Why aren't you happy at the things I say?   870

MEDEA

It is nothing. I was thinking of my children.

JASON

Don't worry. I shall see them well set up.

MEDEA

I shall try to be brave, not mistrust what you say;
But we women are the weaker sex, born weepers.

JASON

Why so unhappy, lady, for these children?

MEDEA

I am their mother. When you prayed that they might live,
Compassion came, and said, "Will it be so?"

For what you came here to discuss with me,
Part has been said, the rest remains to say.
Since the king thinks good to send me from the land,   880
I too think it is good, and I acknowledge it,
Not to embarrass you or the authorities
By staying. I am not welcome in this house.
Yes, I will leave this country, go to exile;
But that your hand alone may rear my sons,
I pray you, beg the king to let them stay.

JASON
I doubt I will succeed, but I must try.

MEDEA
Then you must tell your new wife, the princess,
To beg her father to remit their banishment.

JASON
I'll do it. Yes, I think I can persuade her.   890

MEDEA
You will, if she is a woman like the rest of us.
And I shall lend my shoulder to this labor,
And send her gifts more beautiful by far
Than any man has ever seen, I know—
A fine-spun robe, a golden diadem.
My sons shall take them. One of my servants,
Go bring the robes as quickly as you can.
She will be not once blessed but a thousand times,
Having you, the best of men, to be her husband,
And owning ornaments which once the Sun,   900
My father's father gave to his descendants.

(A *servant brings the presents from the house.*)

Here, take this dowry, children, put it in the hands
Of the happy royal bride. She will not think lightly of it.

JASON
What are you doing? Why deprive yourself?
Do you think the royal house lacks robes?

Do you think we have no gold? Keep them,
Don't give them away. If my wife respects me at all,
She will prefer my wish to presents, I can tell you.

MEDEA

Not so; they say that gifts can move the gods.
A piece of gold is worth a thousand speeches.   910
Her luck is in, god give her more of it.
A queen, so young. I'd willingly give my life
To save my sons from banishment, not only gold.
Go to the halls of wealth, my sons, beseech
The new wife of your father and my queen,
And beg her not to send you into exile.
Give her the presents—this is most important—
Into her own hands.
Now hurry; bring your mother back good news
That you have accomplished what she sets her heart on.   920

(*Exeunt* CHILDREN *and* JASON.)

CHORUS

There is no hope now for the children's lives,
No hope any longer; they go to their deaths,
And the bride, poor bride, will accept the gift
Of the crown worked of gold,
And with her own hands make death an adornment
To set in her yellow hair.

The unearthly splendor and grace of the robe
And the crown worked of gold will persuade her to wear them.
She will soon be attired to marry the dead.
Into such a snare is she fallen,   930
Into such deadly fate, poor girl, and will never
Escape from the curse upon her.

And you, unhappy man, bitter bridegroom,
Who make an alliance with kings,
Unknowing you send your sons to their deaths
And bring on your bride the worst of ends.

How are you deceived in your hopes of the future.

And next to theirs we mourn your sorrows,
Unhappy mother of sons,
Who, to repay your husband for leaving   940
Your bed, and going to live with another
Woman, will kill your children.

(*Enter the* TUTOR, *leading the two* CHILDREN.)

TUTOR

Mistress! Your children are reprieved from exile!
The royal bride was pleased to take into her hands
Your gifts, and with your sons is peace.
Why does good fortune leave you so confused?
Why do you turn your face the other way?
Why aren't you happy at the things I say?

MEDEA

Alas.

TUTOR

Your words and mine are out of tune.

MEDEA

Alas again.

TUTOR

Is there some meaning to my words   950
I do not know? Am I wrong to think them good?

MEDEA

You have said what you have said; I do not blame you.

TUTOR

Why do you drop your eyes, begin to weep?

MEDEA

Because there is necessity, old man. The gods
And my pernicious schemings brought this thing to pass.

TUTOR

Be brave; your children will bring you home again.

MEDEA
I shall send others home before they do.

TUTOR
You are not the only mother to lose her children.
Mankind must bear misfortune patiently.

MEDEA
And so shall I. But go inside the house   960
And see about my children's daily needs.

(*Exit* TUTOR.)

My sons, my sons, you have a city now
And home, where when we've said our sad goodbye
You will stay for ever, parted from your mother.
I go in exile to another land
Before I have had the joy of seeing you happy,
Before I have made your marriage beds, and seen
Your brides, and carried torches at your weddings.
My willfulness has brought its own reward.
For nothing did I toil to bring you up,   970
For nothing did I labor, and endure
The pangs I suffered in your hour of birth.
Once I had in you, oh, once, such splendid hopes,
To have you by my side as I grew old
And when I died, your loving arms around me,
What all men long for. This sweet dream is now
Destroyed. When you and I have parted
My life will be forlorn and desolate.
Your loving eyes will never look upon
Your mother again, you go to another life.   980
My sons, my sons, why do you look at me?
Why smile at me the last smile I shall see?
Oh, oh, what shall I do? Women, my heart
Is faltering when I look at their bright eyes.
I cannot do it; I renounce the plans
I made before, my children shall go with me.

Why should I use their sufferings to hurt
Their father, and so doubly hurt myself?
Not I, not I; I renounce my plans.
And yet—what is happening to me? Shall I let   990
My enemies go scot-free and earn their scorn?
Be bold, Medea. Why, what a coward am I
That can allow my mind talk of relenting.
Go in, my children. He who may not be
Present at my sacrifice without sin,
On his own head be it; my hand is firm.

(*She turns to follow the* CHILDREN *into the house, and then
pauses.*)

Do not do this, my heart, do not do this!
Spare them, unhappy heart, let my sons go.
They will live with you in exile and make you glad.
No, by the fiends that dwell in Hell below,   1000
It shall never come to this, that I allow
My sons to be insulted by my enemies.

(*A noise of shouting is heard off-stage.*)

So; it is finished; there is no escape.
The crown is on her head, the royal bride
Is dying in her robes, this I know well.
And I must tread my own unhappy road;
Far worse the road on which I send my sons.
I want to speak to them. Here, children, give
Your mother your hand, let mother hold your hand.
Oh dearest hand, oh lips I hold most dear,   1010
Dear face, and dear bright eyes, may you be happy—
But in another place; your father leaves
You nothing here. Oh, sweet embrace,
The feel of your skin, the scent of your sweet breath;
Go away! Go away! I have no strength
To look on you, my sorrows overwhelm me.
Women, I know what evil I am to do,
But anger has proved stronger than our reason

And from anger all our greatest ills arise.

(*The* CHILDREN *go into the house.*)

CHORUS

I have often allowed my mind   1020
To speculate, enter into arguments
Lying outside a woman's province.
But there is a Muse in women too
To help us to wisdom; not in all,
But look far enough, and you may find a few
On whom the Muse has smiled.

And I say that those men and women
Who do not know what it means to have children
Are blessed above parents in this world.
A child can bring joy, or bitter pain;
What can the childless know of these?   1030
And those whose fortune it is to be barren
Are spared a world of worry.

But we see that those who tend
The delicate plant of youth in their houses
Have care at their side every hour of the day;
How they will bring their children up,
How they will leave them the means to live,
Will they grow up to be good or bad?
There is no way of knowing.

Then the unkindest blow: 1040
Suppose young bodies grow sturdy and strong
To make parents proud; then if Fate decides,
Down goes Death to the house of Hades,
Taking the children's bodies with him.
How should it profit a man, if heaven
Adds this, the bitterest grief, to his sorrows
Only for loving his children?

MEDEA

Friends, I have awaited my fortune this long while,

Anxious to see which way events would turn.
And now I can see one of Jason's servants   1050
Approaching; he is running, out of breath,
Sure sign of some new horror to report.

(*Enter a* MESSENGER.)

MESSENGER
You who have outraged all laws, and done
This dreadful crime; run, run away, Medea!
Take ship or chariot, and do not scorn their aid!

MEDEA
What have I done, that I should run away?

MESSENGER
The royal bride is dead, and with her
Her father Creon; it was your poisons killed them.

MEDEA
You tell a glorious tale. From this time on
I'll number you among my friends and benefactors.   1060

MESSENGER
Are you in your right mind? Have you gone insane,
To work the ruin of the royal house
And laugh, and not be afraid of what I tell you?

MEDEA
There is a great deal I could say
To answer you. Do not be hasty, friend,
But tell me how they died. My pleasure will
Be doubled, if their deaths were horrible.

MESSENGER
When the two children, your sons, came with their father
And presented themselves at the house where the bride lived,
We servants, who sympathized with your misfortunes,   1070
Were glad, and rumor soon buzzed about the house
That you had patched up the old quarrel with your husband.
Some kissed their hands, and some

Their golden heads; and I was so delighted
I followed the children to the women's quarters.
Our mistress—her we honor in your place—
Only had eyes for Jason, and didn't see
The children, when they came in at first.
And then she turned her pretty head the other way,
Angry they should have been let in. But Jason   1080
Tried to pacify her anger and resentment
And said, "You must not be at odds with friends.
Stop sulking, turn your head this way again;
You must believe your husband's friends are yours.
Accept their gifts, and supplicate your father
To reprieve the boys from exile, for my sake."
When she saw the finery, she couldn't hold out longer,
But did everything he asked. Before the children
And their father had gone far outside the house
She took the pretty robe and put it on,   1090
And set the golden crown around her curls,
Arranging them before a shining mirror
And smiling at her ghostly image there.
Then she stood up, and left the throne, and trod
Her white feet delicately round the room,
Delighted with the gifts, and every now and then
She made a leg and studied the effect.
And then there was a sight that scared us all:
Her color goes, she stumbles sideways, back
Towards the throne, and hardly stops herself   1100
From falling on the floor.
Then some old waiting maid, who must have thought
The fit was sent by Pan, or by some god,
Began to pray; and then she saw her mouth
All white with running froth, the eyeballs starting from
Their sockets, and her body pale and bloodless; and then
She screamed so loud the screaming drowned the prayer.
Someone went straight away to fetch
Her father, someone to her new husband,

To tell them what was happening to the bride, 1110
And the house rang everywhere with noise of running feet.
Already, in the time a practised runner
Could run a hundred yards, the princess
Recovered from her speechless, sightless swoon
And screamed in anguish. It was terrible;
From two directions the pain attacked her.
The golden circlet twining round her hair
Poured forth a strange stream of devouring fire,
And the fine-spun robe, the gift your children gave her,
Had teeth to tear the poor girl's pretty skin. 1120
She left the throne and fled burning through the room,
Shaking her head this way and that,
Trying to dislodge the crown, but it was fixed
Immovably, and when she shook her hair
The flames burnt twice as fiercely.
Then, overcome with pain, she fell to the ground.
Only her father would have recognized her.
Her eyes had lost their settled look, her face
Its natural expression, and the blood
Dripped from her head to mingle with the fire. 1130
The flesh dropped from her bones like pine-tears, torn
By the unseen power of the devouring poison,
We saw, and shuddered; no-one dared
To touch the corpse, we had her fate for warning.
But her old father, who knew nothing of what had happened,
Came running in, and flung himself on the body,
Began to weep, and flung his arms around her,
And kissed her, crying "Oh, unhappy child,
What god has killed you so inhumanly?
Who takes you from me, from the grave of my 1140
Old age? If I could die with you, my child!"
And then he stopped his tears and lamentations
And tried to raise his old body up again,
But clung fast to the robe, as ivy clings
To laurel branches. Then there was a ghastly struggle,

He trying to raise himself from off his knees,
She holding him down; and when he pushed her off
He tore the aged flesh from off his bones.
And then he fought no more; the poor old man
Gave up the ghost, the struggle was too much for him.   1150
The bodies of the princess and her father
Lie side by side, a monument to grief.
Your part in this affair is none of my business.
You will find your own escape from punishment.
Life is a shadow; I have thought so often,
And I am not afraid to say that those
Who seem wise among men, and accomplished talkers,
Must pay the heaviest penalty of all.
No man is happy. He might grow more prosperous
Than other men, if fortune comes his way,   1160
But happy he can never be.

(*Exit.*)

CHORUS

This is the day of heaven's visitation
On Jason, and he has deserved it richly.
But we have only tears for your misfortune,
Poor child of Creon, who must go to Hades
Because of Jason's wedding.

MEDEA

Women, my task is fixed: as quickly as possible
To kill my children and to fly this land,
And not by hesitation leave my sons
To die by other hands more merciless.   1170
Whatever happens, they must die; and since they must,
I, who first gave them life, shall give them death.
Come, steel yourself, my heart; why do you hesitate
To do this dreadful thing which must be done?
Come, my unhappy hand, take up the sword
And go to where life's misery begins.
Do not turn coward; think not of your children,

How much you loved them, how you bore them; no,
For this one day forget you are a mother;
Tomorrow you may weep. But though you kill them, yet   1180
You love them still; and my poor heart is broken.

(*She goes into the house.*)

CHORUS
Earth and all-seeing light of the Sun,
Look down, look down on a woman destroyed
Before she raises her murderous hand
Against her babes. From a golden age
Was she born, and we fear divine blood
Will be shed by mortals. Restrain her, great light
Of heaven, hold her back, drag her forth from the house,
This accursed murderess driven by furies.
Did you toil for your sons in vain, did you labor   1190
For nothing to bring your darlings to birth
When you left behind you the angry straits
Where ships are crushed in the grim grey rocks?
Why has their weight of anger fallen
Upon your heart, this lust for the kill?
The death of kindred is mortals' curse
And heaven sends sorrows meet for the murderers,
Calamities falling upon the house.

(*The* CHILDREN *are heard screaming inside the house.*)
Do you hear them? Do you hear the children crying?
Oh wretched woman, woman,possessed.   1200

FIRST CHILD
What shall I do? How avoid my mother's hand?

SECOND CHILD
I cannot tell, dear brother; we are dying.

CHORUS
Shall we enter the house? We ought to stop
The murder of the children.

FIRST CHILD

Help us in heaven's name, in our necessity.

SECOND CHILD

The sword is near, and death is closing round us.

CHORUS

Woman, you must have a heart of stone
Or iron, that can kill with your own hand
The fruit of your own womb.

One woman, one woman only   1210
I have heard of before this time
Who laid hands on her darling children—
The heaven-demented Ino
Whom Hera made mad, and drove abroad.
And because of her children's dying
The wretched mother drowned,
Leaping from cliff to water
To join her two sons in death.
What worse could the world still hold?
Oh, women, how many sorrows begin   1220
In your bed; what a count of ills
You have brought to mankind already.

(*Enter* JASON.)

JASON

You women, standing close beside the house,
Is she indoors, Medea, that has done
This dreadful crime, or has she taken flight?
She needs must hide herself beneath the earth
Or raise herself on wings to heaven's height
To escape the vengeance of the royal house.
How can she think, when she has killed the king,
That she can escape out of this house unharmed?   1230
It is not her I am thinking of, but my sons;
I leave her to the people she has wronged,
But I am here to save my children's lives
For fear my kinsmen may intend some harm to me

In vengeance for the mother's bloody murder.

CHORUS
Jason, you do not know the full extent
Of your sorrows, or you would not have spoken so.

JASON
What is it? Does she want to kill me too?

CHORUS
Your sons are dead; it was their mother killed them.

JASON
What do you say? You have destroyed me, woman.   1240

CHORUS
You have no children now; remember them.

JASON
Where did she kill them? In the house or outside?

CHORUS
Unbar the door and you will see their bodies.

JASON
What are you waiting for, men? Unbar the doors,
Break them down, so that I may see this double blow,
My dead sons, and she whose blood will pay for theirs.

(MEDEA *appears above the roof of the house in a fiery chariot
drawn by snakes, clasping the bodies of her children.*)

MEDEA
Why hammer on the doors, and try to unbar them,
Seeking the bodies and their murderess?
No need of that. If you want anything from me,
Say what you wish; your hand will never touch me,   1250
So strong the chariot my father's father,
The Sun, gave me to keep away my enemies.

JASON
Abomination! Woman more than any other
Hateful to heaven and to all mankind.
You dared, their mother, thrust the sword

Into their bodies, rob me of my sons,
And show yourself before the world when you
Had done this foul and most abominable of murders?
Your death must pay for this. Oh, now I know
What I did not see before, it was a fatal curse   1260
To bring you from your foreign land to Greece,
Traitor to your father and the land that reared you.
The gods have turned your fury on my head.
You killed your own brother there at your hearthside
Before you set foot on our good ship's deck,
And that was your beginning; married to
The man you see before you, mother of his sons,
Because I left you, you have killed your children.
There is no woman throughout Greece would dare
Do such a thing, and these I overlooked   1270
To marry you, my ruin and my curse.
No woman, but a lioness, more fierce by nature
Than Tyrrhenian Scylla. I could go on abusing you
Forever, and not touch you; such hardness were you born with.
Go, foul woman, children's murderess;
My part to stay and weep for my misfortunes.
No new-wed bride with whom to share my joy,
No children whom I fathered and brought up
To live with me; I have no children.

MEDEA

There is a great deal that I could have said   1280
To answer you, if heaven did not know
How we have dealt with each other, you and I.
Did you think you could desert my marriage bed,
Make me your laughing stock, and still live happy?
Neither your queen nor Creon your new father
Could banish me from Corinth with impunity.
So call me lioness if you will, call me
A Scylla haunting the Tyrrhenian rocks,
I tore your heart for you, and you deserved it.

JASON

You too have paid; you hurt yourself as much.   1290

MEDEA

I do, but gain by it, so do not laugh.

JASON

Oh children, what a mother you have found.

MEDEA

Oh children, dying from your father's malady.

JASON

It was not my hand that killed them; do not say that.

MEDEA

No, your defiance, and your second marriage.

JASON

You make my marriage an excuse for murder?

MEDEA

You think it is a little thing for women?

JASON

For decent women. You think bad of everything.

MEDEA

Your sons are dead, and this will tear your heart.

JASON

My sons live still as curses on your head.   1300

MEDEA

The gods know who began this misery.

JASON

They know then your abominable mind.

MEDEA

You are detestable; I hate your bitter tongue.

JASON

I yours. We have an easy remedy, to part.

MEDEA

How then? What shall I do? I too am eager.

JASON

Give me my sons to bury and to mourn.

MEDEA

No! I shall bury them with my own hands,
Taking them to the Mountain-Mother's shrine
To ensure their tomb will keep its dignity
Untouched by enemies. I will inaugurate   1310
A solemn rite and festival in this land
Of Sisyphus, for future time to expiate
This impious murder; then I go to Erechtheus' land
To live with Aegeus, son of Pandion.
And you will meet the base death you deserve,
Crushed by a relic of your ship, the Argo,
Now you have wept the end of this new wedding.

JASON

May Erinys and bloody Justice
Avenge the death of my children.

MEDEA

What god, what power, will listen to you,   1320
False swearer, betrayer of friends?

JASON

Foul woman, children's murderess.

MEDEA

Go home, and bury your dead.

JASON

I go, with two sons to mourn for.

MEDEA

You will not miss them yet; wait till you are older.

JASON

My darling children.

MEDEA

                  Not yours but mine.

JASON

                And yet you killed them.

MEDEA

                            To give you pain.

JASON
Oh, how I long to kiss
The soft lips of my children.

MEDEA
You would fondle and talk to them now,
Then you rejected them.   1330

JASON
In heaven's name let me feel
The soft touch of my children's bodies.

MEDEA
No, you are wasting your breath.

(*Exit.*)

JASON
Zeus, do you hear how she mocks me,
How she tortures me, this accursed
Lioness, slayer of children?
But with what little power is left me
I call upon heaven to see
My sufferings, and summon the gods
To witness how she prevents me   1340
From giving my children burial.
I wish I had never begot them
To see them destroyed by you.

CHORUS
Many things are wrought by Zeus in Olympus
And heaven works much beyond human imagining.
The looked-for result will fail to materialize
While heaven finds ways to achieve the unexpected.
So it has happened in this our story.

NOTES

References are to line numbers

2 *the Clashing Rocks* at the opening of the Bosphorus. In legend one of the chief hazards for the seafarer; they were believed to close on ships passing between them.

63 *Peirene* Called by an ancient traveller "the pride of Corinth," this fountain is still to be seen. Situated in a grotto, richly provided by later patrons with arches and seats, it gave not only water but shade, and was a popular meeting-place for the citizens.

270 *No sensible man . . .* Euripides puts into Medea's mouth a speech bitterly descriptive of his own situation. His bold views, his association with some of the most notorious freethinkers of his time, and his habit of working in solitude, did not endear him to his fellow-citizens. The scurrilous stories in the ancient "Life" of Euripides and the cruel caricatures in Aristophanes' comedies reflect the antagonism which such behavior aroused. He was eventually forced to leave Athens and end his life as an expatriate.

372 *Hecate* In one of her aspects the goddess of witchcraft, and so adopted by Medea as a patron deity.

380 *Sisyphean wedding* Sisyphus was the legendary founder of the earliest settlement on the site of Corinth. A promoter of navigation and commerce, he was regarded by tradition as fraudulent and avaricious. See *Cyclops* l. 131, where he is jocularly referred to as the "father" of the wily Odysseus.

489 *Tempers run high* Perhaps the best way of regarding these brief choral interjections, in Euripides often platitudinous, is as a mechanical expedient. The actors were masked and declaimed their parts in a highly artificial style. All parts were played by men, and even at this time there was little, if any, attempt to make a vocal distinction between male and female characters. Thus it would sometimes be difficult for the audience to distinguish where one character stopped speaking and the other began. The author has experienced a similar difficulty in hearing an unfamiliar opera in the Theatre of Herodes Atticus; it was often impossible to tell which of a

group of soloists was singing at any one time. Here the choral
interjection clearly marks the division of speeches, and gives
the audience time to refocus its attention. It can safely be cut
in modern performance.

496 *Cypris* Aphrodite, Goddess of Love.

633 *earth's prophetic center.* Zeus, according to the myth, sent
two eagles flying from each end of the earth; they met over
Delphi, which was thus established as the center point, and
marked by a pointed stone (*omphalos,* navel) in the oracular
shrine.

638 *no stranger to the marriage bond.* Aegeus had already
married twice.

644 *not to loosen* . . . The Delphic Oracle is typically ambiguous.
Aegeus is commanded "not to loosen the wineskin's hanging foot"—that is, not to engage in sexual intercourse—
until he reaches his "ancestral hearth." He naturally takes
this to mean Athens. But on his way home he stopped at
Troezen and lay with Aethra, who bore him a son. Euripides
is referring here to a tradition whereby Troezen was already
associated with Athens; thus the "ancestral hearth" could
apply equally well to either place, and the oracle is proved
correct.

775 *Since you have taken me* . . . Here the awkwardness of the
chorus becomes apparent. Euripides is compelled to take their
presence into account and make Medea divulge her plans to
them; though they object, the exigencies of the plot forbid
them to interfere. Euripides has given their inaction a bare
plausibility by making Medea, earlier in the play, swear them
to secrecy.

788 *Erechtheus* Mythical founder of the Athenian people. The
chorus try to divert Medea from her purpose by dwelling on
the glory and sanctity of Athens. How could such a city receive a murderess? This provides an opportunity for a burst of
patriotic sentiment.

895 A *fine-spun robe* The exact repetition of this line from
l. 751 has led some editors to excise it as an interpolation. It
has, however, considerable dramatic point. Jason does not
appreciate the full significance of the phrase, but the chorus
and audience do. This is true dramatic irony.

994 *Go in, my children.* We must imagine the children as
turning to go into the house, and then pausing at the door as
Medea continues to speak.

1164 *But we have only tears* . . . These lines have been dismissed
by some editors as a sentimental interpolation, but they are in
keeping with Euripides' intention. He wishes to stress the
horror of the deaths of Creon and the princess, and by implication the murders of Apsurtos and Pelias. This accounts for
the Grand Guignol nature of the Messenger's speech, which
violates all the customary restraint of Greek tragedy. Euripides
is concerned to show the true nature of violence, and to condemn the acceptance of such episodes in the traditional
stories. Thus the chorus makes a clear distinction. Jason deserved his punishment, but the princess did not; she, like
Medea's brother, has been sacrificed to further a personal
advantage.

1201 *What shall I do?* Although he is forced to work within
the old conventions, Euripides often contrives to give them a
new twist. Tragedy was allowed only three speaking actors;
thus the children must be *personae mutae*, silent characters,
as long as they are on the stage. But Euripides uses their un-
speaking presence to increase the pathos of their plight. Every
time we see them, we wonder if it will be the last. Note how
Euripides gives the final twist by postponing their final exit
(see l. 994 and note). When we do hear them, it is in the
moment of their death.

1210 *One woman* . . . This chorus serves a dual purpose. First,
it increases the excitement of her predicament. In drawing this
parallel between Medea's crime and Ino's, Euripides seems to
depart from the usual version, in which Ino saw one of her
sons killed by his father and leapt into the sea with the other,
for one in which Ino killed both sons and then leapt into the
sea herself. The parallel, of course, is not as exact as the
chorus thinks. Medea does not die, though the chorus sees this
as inevitable, and so does Jason when he appears. The escape
in the dragon chariot thus comes as a great surprise.

The chorus also provides a welcome relief from the high
tragedy that has gone before. The tension has mounted
higher and higher, to culminate in Medea's speech of decision

and the dying screams of the children. Euripides now gives his audience a moment to recuperate.

1244 *What are you waiting for?* Euripides once more gives a new and exciting twist to an old formula. Such commands to "unbar the door" are customarily followed by the revelation of the *ekkyklema*, a wheeled platform bearing a tableau of the dead bodies. The audience, hearing the familiar words, would have their gaze riveted on the central door. Then, from above, comes a cry, and Medea is seen on the roof of the stage building. Euripides has performed a theatrical conjuring trick, distracting the audience's attention to one point while he brings in Medea at another.

1254 *Hateful to heaven* . . . An exact repetition of l. 437 and thus excised by most editors. But it emphasizes the exact counterbalancing of the two halves of the play. Earlier, Medea said this of Jason; now, Jason says it of Medea. Their positions have been completely reversed.

1273 *Scylla* The mythical monster, familiar from the *Odyssey*, who lived in a sea-cave and preyed on passing ships.

1318 *Mountain-mother's shrine* Euripides likes to link his plays to some familiar rite or festival—here, to the worship of Hera.

1316 *Crushed by a relic* . . . There were two versions of Jason's death. According to one, he was sleeping under the beached Argo, now old and rotten, when the timbers collapsed on his head. According to the other, he had dedicated the stem of his ship in the temple of Hera; one day, as he was visiting the shrine, it fell down and killed him. Euripides seems to be following the second version.

1344 *Many things are wrought* . . . A stock epilogue, which appears at the end of several plays.

Cyclops / EURIPIDES

INTRODUCTION

1. THE PLAY

Cyclops is a slight play, and requires only a slight introduction. It is an example of a minor Greek dramatic form, the satyr play. Satyr-plays were performed as light relief in the dramatic festivals, following the morning's offerings of three tragedies, and one was required from each participating tragedian. They were short, and predominantly humorous in tone—often broadly so. So far as we can see, they consisted of burlesque versions of popular myths and legends; often the theme would be loosely related to the tragedies that had gone before. The chorus was composed of satyrs, and the shaggy and obese Silenus, father of the satyrs, is a recurring figure. The function of satyr play was to entertain, and we must not expect depth of characterization or inspiring thoughts, but merely a simple story amusingly told. As with tragedy, our loss of the Greek music is a severe disadvantage. We know enough about the typical dances of a satyr-play to realize that this must have been a spectacular and fast-moving show, always vigorous and often obscene. Greek dancing was highly mimetic, and the opening chorus of Cyclops shows how effectively mimesis was used. The chorus go through a dance-pattern representing the actions of herding a large and unruly flock. It need hardly be said that the animals themselves are present only in the minds of the spectators.

Aeschylus' work in this genre was famous in his own time, but has come down to us only in isolated fragments. These contain, however, some remarkably tender and sensitive passages, enough to show us that his reputation was deserved. Enough of Sophocles' Searching Satyrs remains to allow us to reconstruct the plot; it tells of Hermes' theft of Apollo's cattle, and his appeasement of the older god by a gift of the newly invented lyre. Euripides' *Cyclops*, however, is the only satyr play to come down to us entire. It is therefore something of a literary curiosity, and has tended for this reason to arouse an interest disproportionate to its merits.

We do not know when *Cyclops* was written, and supposed allusions or parodies in other plays will not bear investigation. About the subject matter, however, we know a great deal. The story is taken from the ninth book of the *Odyssey*, and Euripides has reproduced the main incidents of Homer's account in dramatic form. There are inevitable changes. Some incidents must be telescoped and others expanded, and justification must be found for the presence of the satyr chorus. A prologue, put into the mouth of Silenus, links the Odysseus episode to a completely unrelated story of the adventures of Dionysus. Other changes are purely mechanical. The action must be transferred from inside the cave to outside, and the flock of sheep under which the Homeric Odysseus and his companions make their escape must go, to be replaced by a far less ingenious expedient.

The play is in fact so derivative that we may well ask whether the high opinion formed of it by some scholars is justified. There are several signs of hasty composition. Nevertheless, the story is still entertaining. Even without the music, the play is still full of life and good humor, and could well stand more frequent revival than it has enjoyed in the past.

2. THE TRANSLATION

THE reader will observe marked differences between the method of translation used for *Cyclops* and the more orthodox rendering into iambics of *Medea*. The reasons for this are twofold. As *Cyclops* is so different in character from any other Greek play that we have, it seemed that this difference ought to be brought out somehow in the English translation. Also, the satyr play represents an earthier and more primitive concept of drama than the formal and elaborate tragedy. A meter that would convey this quality was therefore desirable; and the present translation employs the later medieval alliterative verse form, in the manner of *Piers Plowman*. This has several advantages for the translator from Greek, notably in maintaining a strict discipline without imposing an arbitrary length on the line. It is hoped that the sporadic use of rhyme, and the occasional contrast between the dignified alliterative meter and the language of the street will convey that feeling of mock-heroic burlesque which is of the essence of satyr-play. The version was first written for a production in which the choruses were set to Welsh folk-music. Thus, particularly in the opening chorus, the order of the Greek has been rearranged to suit a more modern verse arrangement. As even without the music this arrangement seems by no means an inappropriate way of conveying the feeling of the piece, it has been retained here.

CHARACTERS

SILENUS, father to the Satyrs
CHORUS of Satyrs
ODYSSEUS
POLYPHEMUS, the CYCLOPS
Sailors of Odysseus

The action takes place before the cave of POLYPHEMUS, *on the coast of Sicily.* SILENUS *emerges from the cave, carrying a rake, and grumbling to himself.*

SILENUS

From boyhood, Bacchus, when my blood was hot,
My whole life long have I labored in your service
And paid for my passion with a thousand pains.
First Hera's fury forced you to fly
From the mountains, unmindful of the nymphs that nursed you;
Then the fight we fought with the giants, our foes,
When I stood at your shoulder spear in hand
And caught Enceladon's shield a crack
That dropped him dead—what's that? I was dreaming?
Why, Bacchus, I brought the booty to show you.   10
But the past was child's play to my present plight.
For there were some Tuscans, pirates by trade
Whom Hera aroused, and put it in their heads
To carry you off to the ends of the earth.
When they brought me the news, I embarked with my boys
In pursuit of the pirates; I perched in the stern
To steer the ship straight, while my sons at their oars
Sweated and strained, and stirred the grey waters
To foam with their flailing, as we followed you, lord.
But, as our course carried us close off Malea,   20
Came a keen east wind, that encompassed our ship
And cast up the crew on the cliffs of Etna.
Here the sea-god's sons, the one-eyed Cyclopes
Haunt the hollow caves; human flesh is their food.
Such a creature caught us, and kept us for slaves
Immured in his cavern; men call our master,
This fiend, Polyphemus. Our feasting forgotten
We serve this Cyclops and shepherd his flock.
My sons spend their days on the spur of the hill,
My young with his young, his ewes and his lambs,   30
While I must stay inside, to sweep the cave,

Fill troughs for his flock, and furnish the table
With the monstrous meals that my master requires.
But I have my orders, obey them I must,
To clean the cavern with this clumsy rake,
To fork the floor over and free it from filth,
And welcome the wanderer, when he returns,
To a spotless sty for himself and his sheep.
I can see my sons, with their sheep before them,
Coming home from the hills. Why, what do I hear?   40
The din of dancing feet, as in days of old,
When we leapt in delight with Bacchus our leader
To the lilt of the lyre, and arms linked together
Sang sweet serenades to Althea's house.

(*Enter the* CHORUS *of* SATYRS.)

CHORUS
Billy boy, where are you biding?
Come from the mountain-side, come.
Up among the hill-tops hiding,
Come from the mountain-side, come.
Shelter here from bitter weather,
Fol lol la dee i do,   50
Wind and storm will harm you never,
Fol lol la dee i do.

Come you down, my horned sweeting,
Come to your children, boy, come.
Can't you hear your kids a-bleating?
Come to your children, boy, come.
By the river gently flowing,
Fol lol la dee i do,
Where the grass is greener growing,
Fol lol la dee i do.   60

You are proud, my pretty prancer,
Come, royal billy-goat, come.
Nobly born, and will not answer,

Come royal billy goat, come.
Soon your flocks will all disown you,
Fol lol la dee i do,
Come away before I stone you,
Fol lol la dee i do.

Come, be milked, your lambs lack feeding,
Come to the milking-pail, come.   70
Comfort from their dams are needing,
Come to the milking-pail, come.
Such a bleating they've been keeping,
Fol lol la dee i do,
Woken from their long day's sleeping,
Fol lol la dee i do.

Leave the grassy plain behind you,
Come from the pasture-land, come.
Get you home and never mind you,
Come from the pasture-land, come.   80
Sleep now in your cavern stable,
Fol lol la dee i do,
You have eaten all you're able,
Fol lol la dee i do.

Here is little comfort for us,
Gone are the happy days, gone.
Gone the dance and gone the chorus,
Gone are the happy days, gone.
Golden wine no longer sipping
Fol lol la dee i do,   90
By the fountains gently rippling,
Fol lol la dee i do.

Hear our song
Queen of love
From above!
Once I sought to find you;
Hail, queen of love!

And sported with your maidens fair
So white of limb and gold of hair,
Hail, queen of love!   100

Bacchus lord,
Where are you
Roaming now,
Tossing golden tresses?
Where are you, lord?
For cloak a rotting skin I have
And toil as one-eyed Cyclops' slave
Far from you, lord.

SILENUS

Be quiet, my boys; have them bring the flocks
As quick as they can to the cavern's shelter.   110

CHORUS

Make haste, good hearts. Why such hurry, father?

SILENUS

I see a Greek ship come ashore close by
And the master mariners, commander and all,
Coming to our cave, with casks on their shoulders
To fill with fresh water, and forage for food
In the baskets they bear. But who can they be?
Poor fools! Does none of them know our lord
Polyphemus' fame? They follow a path
Unsafe for strangers, steering their steps
To the arms of an ogre who eats men alive.   120
Hold your tongues all; for so may we hear
Whence they sailed to Sicily, and Etna's shores.

(*Enter* ODYSSEUS *and several of his men, carrying baskets and barrels.*)

ODYSSEUS

Friends, where can we find fresh water, I pray?
We are dry, and would drink; and do any desire
To sell hungry sailors a sackful of food?

But what have we here? Bacchus' hidey-hole, sure!
A cave with a satyr-crowd sitting beside it!
I'll go to their grandpa and give him good-day.

SILENUS
Welcome, stranger; tell us your country and name.

ODYSSEUS
King Odysseus, from Ithaca.

SILENUS
                                        Far is your fame!   130
As sharp as a handspike, old Sisyphus' son.

ODYSSEUS
You know my name; no need to make fun.

SILENUS
What shore did you sail from for Sicily, pray?

ODYSSEUS
From Troy, when we'd turned all the Trojans away.

SILENUS
What, had you forgotten the way to your door?

ODYSSEUS
A storm seized our ship, and drove us ashore.

SILENUS
Poor soul, the same fate happened to me.

ODYSSEUS
Why, were you too swept in from the sea?

SILENUS
Pursuing the pirates that stole Bacchus away.

ODYSSEUS
Where have we landed? Who lives here, pray?   140

SILENUS
That's Sicily's summit, Etna, my son.

ODYSSEUS
But where is the city? Walls are there none.

SILENUS
Nothing here but hills, all empty of men.

ODYSSEUS
The land is left to the wild beasts then?

SILENUS
Cyclopes, who have no houses, but caves.

ODYSSEUS
Who's their king? Or do they scorn to be slaves?

SILENUS
They're shepherds; for no man a thought do they give.

ODYSSEUS
Do they sow corn here? Or how do they live?

SILENUS
On mutton and cheese, and milk from their sheep.

ODYSSEUS
And do they the vine in due honor keep?   150

SILENUS
Not at all; this country is empty of cheer.

ODYSSEUS
Are they kindly? Are wanderers welcome here?

SILENUS
They love them. They like nothing better to eat.

ODYSSEUS
What! Cannibals, feasting on human meat?

SILENUS
They slaughter each stranger who ventures near.

ODYSSEUS
Where is this Cyclops? Don't tell me he's here.

SILENUS
Hunting in the hills with his hounds today.

ODYSSEUS
Do you know what you must do, to help us away?

SILENUS
No, but there's nothing I wouldn't do for you.

ODYSSEUS
We're famished, so feed us; that's what you must do.   160

SILENUS
I told you, we've nothing to trade but meat.

ODYSSEUS
Starvation's good sauce, and sailors must eat.

SILENUS
There's curdled cheese, and milk if you're dry.

ODYSSEUS
Then show them; I like to inspect what I buy.

SILENUS
How much will you pay for this food of mine?

ODYSSEUS
No money, but god's own gift of wine.

SILENUS
Oh wonderful word! For years I've had none.

ODYSSEUS
A present from Maron, Apollo's son.

SILENUS
The babe I brought up, and carried about?

ODYSSEUS
The god's very own son, you need have no doubt.   170

SILENUS
Is it on board ship, or here with you now?

ODYSSEUS
In this very wineskin, old fellow; so!

SILENUS
There's not enough here to fill my mouth.

ODYSSEUS
More than two bladdersful, that's the truth.

SILENUS

O fountain of bliss! O well of delight!

ODYSSEUS

Shall I pour some neat, to whet your appetite?

SILENUS

Fair enough; we will bind our bargain so.

ODYSSEUS

This wine-skin has a cup in tow.

SILENUS

Pour it out; I've almost forgotten the way.

ODYSSEUS

There!

SILENUS

   Heavens above, what a gorgeous bouquet!   180

ODYSSEUS

Do you see what I mean?

SILENUS

        Not see, but smell.

ODYSSEUS

Then try if the taste is entrancing as well.

SILENUS

Oho, I must dance! Bacchus sounds the note!

ODYSSEUS

Did it slip so sweetly down your throat?

SILENUS

It trickled right down to the tips of my toes.

ODYSSEUS

I've coins here too, if you'd care for those.

SILENUS

You can keep your money; just open the skin.

ODYSSEUS

Very well! Fetch your mutton and cheeses in.

SILENUS

You may have your meat; my master be hanged!
I am so mad for a mouthful more   190
I'd sell you the sheep of all the Cyclopes,
Yes, consign them to sink in the sea below,
Could I once drink deep and drive care from my brow.
The man must be mad whom drink does not make merry.
For wine is the well of all worldly desires,
Of laughter and love, the delights of the dance,
Of oblivion sweet. Then shall not my lips
Caress such richness, and rid me of fear
For the stupid Cyclops and his single eye?

(SILENUS *goes into the cave to bring out the cheese and meat.*)

CHORUS

Odysseus, we satyrs would speak with you.   200

ODYSSEUS

Then ask of me freely, as friend to friend.

CHORUS

Did you take Troy, and treacherous Helen too?

ODYSSEUS

And plundered and burned all Priam's possessions.

CHORUS

When you took her, why didn't you take it in turns
To give her the treatment she deserved?
The traitress! So taken with Paris' fine trousers
And the collar of gold that gleamed at his throat
That she left Menelaus, most lovable of men,
In the lurch, all alone. I believe it were better
There were no women—only one for me.   210

(SILENUS *returns, loaded with food.*)

SILENUS

See, here are the lambs you looked for, my lord
Odysseus, the darlings of bleating dams,

And curds from the churn, and cheeses in plenty.
Now get out of this cave, as quickly as you can,
And give us the glory of the grape to cheer us.

(*A roar is heard off-stage.*)

Heaven help us! The Cyclops is here! What now?

ODYSSEUS
Good father, we're finished! Where can we fly?

SILENUS
You can creep in the cave to escape his eye.

ODYSSEUS
It's a senseless scheme to step straight in the snare.

SILENUS
I'm telling the truth; many tunnels in there.   220

ODYSSEUS
Shall I fly from one foe, and surrender the fame
Of my triumphs at Troy? Why, time and again
I stood under shield against Trojans a score!
If death is our due, we will die without shame,
And if we live still, let our fame live longer.

(*Enter the* CYCLOPS. SILENUS *disappears hastily into the cave.*)

CYCLOPS
Back to your business! Come, bustle about!
Making merry indeed! You serve Bacchus no more;
No clashing of cymbals or kettledrums here.
How are my lambs? Are they locked inside,
Taking milk from their mothers? And have you made   230
The cheeses to cram my crates brimful?
Come, speak. Are you dumb? Let's see if my stick
Can untie your tongue. Take your eyes from the ground.

CHORUS
Why, we're looking at Zeus aloft in the sky;
I can see all the stars, and Orion himself.

CYCLOPS
Have you made my meal ready, may I ask?

CHORUS
As long as your appetite's up to the task.

CYCLOPS
Have you put plenty of milk in my dish?

CHORUS
You can drink a whole barrelful, lord, if you wish.

CYCLOPS
Of ewe's milk, or cow's, or a mixture of these?   240

CHORUS
Whatever you wish; don't drink me as well, please!

CYCLOPS
My stomach would soon know if I swallowed you;
Your kicks and capers would cut me to pieces.

(*He sees* ODYSSEUS *and the sailors.*)

What crowd is this at my cavern door?
Have pirates or thieves come to plunder our homes?
And look at these lambs—my lambs, if you please—
Brought from the cave with their bodies bound
And casks of cheese! Here comes the old man,
Beaten and bloody, his bald pate broken!

(SILENUS *enters, made up to look as if he has been beaten.*)

SILENUS
I'm punched and I'm pummelled, poor wretch that I am.   250

CYCLOPS
Who was it who hammered your head, old man?

SILENUS
These strangers! I sought to stop them from stealing.

CYCLOPS
Rob a god, a god's son? Don't they know with whom they're
dealing?

SILENUS

I threatened the thieves, but they thrived in their task
And swallowed your cheese, though I sought to stop them,
Laid your lambs on their shoulders, and led them away.
They boasted they'd bind a long rope round your belly
And tie you up tight, and tear out your guts,
And bare your back to the bone with whipping,
Then bring you home bound in the hold, and hire you   260
To toil in a mine, or turn a treadmill.

CYCLOPS

Is that so? Then sharpen my knives on the stone
And fetch me a faggot to light my fire.
I shall kill this crew, and cook them on the coals,
And have them hot to ease my hunger.
Some I shall roast, and some I shall stew;
For I am so weary of wild game
And have fed so long on lion and deer
I am fairly famished for human flesh!

SILENUS

When you have the same dishes for dinner each day   270
A change is a blessing, and brings new cheer.
It's some time since strangers were seen at your door.

ODYSSEUS

Come, Cyclops, let strangers speak in their turn.
We were famished for food, and to find a market
Set foot ashore and found your cave.
He sold us your sheep for a skin of wine,
And when he had tasted a tot of our treasure
Offered us all of his own accord.
He found them freely, and we did not force him.
There is no truth at all in the tales he tells;   280
He's convicted of selling your goods on the sly.

SILENUS

Go to hell!

ODYSSEUS
　　Most certainly, if I lie.

SILENUS
Cyclops, I swear by Poseidon your sire,
By mighty Triton, by Calypso too,
By Nereus and his nymphs, by the fish unnumbered
That have their home in the holy waters,
O Cyclops my sweeting, I swear by all these,
Little master mine, not a mite of your store
Did I sell to these strangers. A curse on my sons,
Much as I love the dear lads, if I lie!   290

CHORUS
A curse on yourself! I saw you at it,
Trading with the travelers. If I don't tell the truth,
A curse on my father! Don't wrong these strangers.

CYCLOPS
You lie in your teeth; he is telling the truth.
Rhadamanthus himself is not more to be trusted.
I will question this crew. Where did you come from?
In what land do you live? To what state owe allegiance?

ODYSSEUS
We are Ithacans born; we travel from Troy.
When the city was sacked, we were seized by a storm
That swept us ashore on your seacoast, Cyclops.   300

CYCLOPS
It was you hunted Helen, and haled her home
From Scamander's stream by the city of Troy?

ODYSSEUS
We did, and endured great dangers to get her.

CYCLOPS
What a worthless war—for one woman's sake
To send such a fleet to Phrygia to fight.

ODYSSEUS
God brought it about; blame none among men.

We beseech you, great son of the sea-god your sire,
And pray for your pardon in good plain words.
We have come to your cave as friends; to kill us
And make us your meal is a monstrous crime.   310
For we are the warriors, worthiest lord,
Who fought for your father, and helped to uphold
His shrines in safe keeping on Hellas' far shores.
His temple may stand on Taenarus untouched,
And on Malea's cliffs, secure from all harm.
Safe is Sunium's silver, Athena's store,
And Geraestus, our refuge; we are rid of the shame
That our Phrygian foes had inflicted upon us.
You also may share in these blessings, residing
At our land's far limits, in Etna's lava.   320
And if my arguments do not affect you
It is law among men, and custom demands it,
That castaways craving for kindness and shelter
Should depart dry-apparelled, with presents in their packs,
Not be skewered on spits, like swine from the sty,
Or give their bodies to glut your greed.
We have lost enough lives in the land of Priam,
Which bloated with blood and the bodies of slain
Made widows of wives, made mothers weep,
Stole sons from gray sires; should we who survived   330
Be flung in the fire to fill your foul feast,
Where may a man turn? Be admonished by me:
Repress your proud stomach, repent of your sins,
Give ear to good counsel; our gains full often
Are levelled to loss, when unlawfully won.

SILENUS
Come, hear my counsel; chew him up whole;
Spare not a scrap; if you swallow his tongue
You will be a smooth speech-maker, Cyclops, yourself.

CYCLOPS
The wise have but one god, wealth, little man.

All others are air, and empty talk.   340
The shrines that my father founded on the sea-shore
Can all topple down; why talk to me of these?
I take no thought for the thunders of Zeus
Nor grant him a greater god than I.
I care not what comes; the cause will I show
If you mark well my words. When he wills it to rain
I have a dry dwelling indoors in my cave
Where I feast on roast flesh, or on wild fowl,
And gulp down my gullet a gallon of milk.
So I sprawl on my back, my stomach skywards,   350
And it rumbles, deriding the roar of the thunder.
When the wild winds from Thrace bring winter snow
I wrap my body in beast-skins warm,
Set flame to my fire, and the frost cannot harm me.
The earth each year, if it will or no,
Must furnish fresh pasture to fatten my flocks.
I sacrifice sheep to no man but myself
And to none of the gods but my belly, the greatest.
The wordly wise honor one god alone,
To dine and drink deep every day of your life   360
And let the world pass. These men who make laws
To trouble and tease us, and take up our time
I scorn all such, and shall ever pursue
My spirit's desire by swallowing you.
You will get your gifts, I am not ungracious;
A cauldron to cook you, a fire beneath
And my sire's sea water to stew your bones.
Now step inside, and stand at the altar,
A sight for sore stomachs, to gladden my god.

(*The* CYCLOPS *and* SILENUS *drive the sailors inside the cave.*)

ODYSSEUS
Through perils and pain did I pass at Troy,   370
Through shipwreck and storm, to be stranded now
Aground on a godless ungrateful heart.

Dear daughter of Zeus, do not be deaf to my plea;
Reprieve me, I pray; I am worse oppressed
Than ever at Troy, and touch terror's depths.
And you who sit in the shining stars,
Zeus, god of guests, regard my suffering.
If you look not below, we were wrong to believe
In your godhead, great Zeus; for god is there none.

(*He enters the cave.*)

CHORUS
Come, Cyclops, your gullet gape wide   380
And open your mouth as you may;
The pot is a-simmer inside,
You have a good dinner today!
Your hand you have only to stir,
The strangers await your desire,
Well roasted if so you prefer
Or tastily toasted, so carve any cut you require
Wrapped warm in your rugs by the fire.

Bestow not your dainties on me,
Consume them alone in your pride.   390
Your ship you may sail on the sea,
We never will sail at your side.
This cave would I quit if I might,
This Cyclops who holds us oppressed
On Etna, and feeds with delight
On sacrifice savage and strange, on a banquet unblessed,
The body and bones of his guest.

How horrid his hunger, I say,
To sacrifice men at his hearth
Who pray for protection, and slay   400
All strangers who walk in his path.
This cannibal master of mine,
Inhuman and savage of soul,
On stews and roast dishes will dine,

Will sink his foul teeth in the meat, set his lips to the bowl,
All plucked piping hot from the coal.

(*Enter* ODYSSEUS.)

ODYSSEUS
Zeus, what can I say? I have seen such things—
Like long-ago legends, you could not believe
That mortal men could commit such horrors.

CHORUS
What is it, Odysseus? Has the demon dined   410
And feasted his fill on your faithful friends?

ODYSSEUS
On two; he took us in his hands to test us,
To see which was fattest and most fit for slaughter.

CHORUS
Say on, poor stranger; what did you suffer?

ODYSSEUS
When we came to the cave in the cliff so deep
First he kindled a fire, and then flung on the flames
The helm of an oak, so huge and so heavy
I wonder three wagons could carry the weight.
Then he strewed a soft couch for himself at the hearthside,
A thick pile of pine-needles plucked from the bough,   420
Then took up a tankard ten gallons deep
Brimful with milk from his many flocks.
A fine wooden bowl some four feet wide
And six feet deep he set there beside,
Made the stew-pot sing as it sat on the flames,
Then seized his spits, rough-shaped with a bill-hook,
Their heads hammered hard in the heat of the fire,
And bowls to hold blood from the blows of his cleaver.
When all was arranged in order, he took,
This hell-cook, god-hated, in one huge swing   430
Two men from among us and unmade them both;
One struck on the stewpot till the bronze resounded,

One held by the heel, and hammered his head
On a sharp spur of rock till his brains spilled out.
He seized knife and sliced them, set some to roast
And put some apart in the pot to boil.
I wept as I watched what they underwent
And tiptoed towards them to await their turn.
My friends in their fear, like a flock of poor birds,
Crept into corners, their color all gone.   440
Having feasted his fill on the flesh of my men
He belched a foul blast of breath from his belly
And sat himself down. Then I was inspired
To fetch the wineskin, and fill his cup,
Saying thus: "Cyclops, son of the sea-god,
Drink deep of this draught, Dionysus' child,
The glory of Greece, and the gift of the vine."
All glutted and gorged with his ungodly feast
He seized it, and swilled it down in one swallow,
Then threw up his hands in praise and replied   450
"A fine finish, friend, to a fine feast."
When I looked at him laughing and full of delight
I gave him the goblet again, well knowing
That the wine would overwhelm him, and win me revenge.
Soon he fell to singing, and still I poured
Cup upon cup, till the cockles of his heart
Were warm with the wine. He warbled so loud,
With the moans of my men to make him a chorus,
That the rocks resounded; and I stole forth silently
To seek my salvation, and yours, if you desire it.   460
How say you? Consent you, or consent you not
To fly the foul fiend, and henceforth dwell
With Bacchus and the nymphs in his beautiful halls?
Your father inside has assented; but he
Is weak, and is wooing the wine; he is bound
As fast to the bowl as a bird to a snare,
And his wits are astray. But you are young and strong;
Save me, and restore yourselves to your lord

Dionysus, so different from that devil within.

CHORUS
We would dare a good deal to see that day   470
And escape this cave and the Cyclops' clutches.

ODYSSEUS
Then hear my plan, how I plot to repay
This creature in kind, and contrive your escape.

CHORUS
Then say on, quickly; the Cyclops' death
Is sweeter in my ears than the sound of the harp.

ODYSSEUS
He desires to set out, so steeped is he in wine,
To bid forth his brothers and bring them to the feast.

CHORUS
You will seize him and slay him in some solitary grove,
Or hurl him headlong from a mountain top?

ODYSSEUS
No such thing; my intent is more subtle.   480

CHORUS
Come, tell us; we know you are crafty and clever.

ODYSSEUS
I'll dissuade him from sharing his sport, and say
It were wiser not give such wine away
To the Cyclopes, but keep it to cheer his own heart.
So when the wine has won him, and weighed him with sleep. . . .
The limb of an olive-tree hangs by the wall.
I will sharpen it with my sword, and set it straight
Ablaze in the embers; when the end burns bright
I'll fetch it flaming from the fire, and thrust
The end all hot in the Cyclops' eye,   490
Then set to work as shipwrights do
When boring holes in the beam of a boat
By twirling a drill between two thongs.

So I shall set the stake spinning round
In the Cyclops' eye, and steal his sight.

CHORUS
Hurrah! Hurrah!
Your cunning and craft make me crow with delight.

ODYSSEUS
Then you and my friends, and your father too
I shall bring on board my black-hulled ship
And with new hands to help us we'll hurry away.   500

CHORUS
May I play my part as a priest in this rite
And stand to the stake that will scorch out his eye?
I am longing to lend my hand to this labor.

ODYSSEUS
You must, for to move it is monstrous heavy.

CHORUS
I would move the weight of a hundred wagons
Could I steal the cursed Cyclops' sight
And burn out his eye with the blazing brand
The way we burn wasps from the trunk of a tree.

ODYSSEUS
Be silent, good souls, for you understand all.
Then wait on my word, who worked this plan.   510
I'll not seek safety by deserting my friends,
Though escape I could, for I quit the cave
Through a rift in the rock, and the rest are within.
Shall I alone live, and relinquish the friends
In whose company I came? It would be a crime.

CHORUS
Who first will take his stand by me
And set his hand to yonder tree
And thrust it boldly, one two three,
To stop his eye a-winking?
So softly, softly, hear his song,   520

He'll sing a different tune 'ere long;
See where he comes, all flushed with wine,
He knows no better, comrades mine,
Let's teach him how to spend his time,
He'll soon be blind, I'm thinking.

(*While the chorus sing, the* CYCLOPS *staggers out of the cave with*
SILENUS. *He is very drunk.*)

Our drinking songs are merry things
With friends to sing the chorus;
Wine will give your spirit wings,
Such joys the grape holds for us.

So clasp you tight your lady fair   530
And love's delights begin, sir;
Stroke her shining golden hair
And softly seek to win her.

CYCLOPS
Oho, so full of wine am I
And heavy with much drinking,
Like a ship that's loaded high
And precious near to sinking.

A glorious night to sing and shout
And dance among the clover;
Brothers, come and help me out—   540
Friend, pass the wineskin over!

CHORUS
Lover, leave your pacing,
See, your bride is coming,
Someone loves us, I can tell; oh, how your eye's a-gleaming!
In the cave are waiting
Bridal torches blazing,
Blossoms red around your head, and kisses warm and pressing!

ODYSSEUS
Come, Cyclops, the god that you drink is my friend.
I'll tell you his tale from beginning to end.

CYCLOPS
What is this Bacchus, a god, my boy?   550

ODYSSEUS
The greatest of gods in giving men joy.

CYCLOPS
I belch him out so, and it cheers me no end.

ODYSSEUS
Why, that's his good nature; he's every man's friend.

CYCLOPS
And how does he like to lodge in a skin?

ODYSSEUS
He's perfectly happy whatever he's in.

CYCLOPS
A skin's no fit suit for a god, that's true.

ODYSSEUS
What's that, if you're happy? Does the skin hurt you?

CYCLOPS
I don't like the skin, but I love what's in it.

ODYSSEUS
Then sit still and drink, and enjoy every minute.

CYCLOPS
Not bring my brothers to share my new wealth?   560

ODYSSEUS
Far better to keep it all to yourself.

CYCLOPS
It were neighborly done to share with my brothers.

ODYSSEUS
You're sure to start squabbles by sharing with others.

CYCLOPS
I'm drunk; don't touch me, leave me alone.

ODYSSEUS
The happiest place for a drunkard is home.

CYCLOPS
The drinker who doesn't like parties is mad.

ODYSSEUS
Far better stay home when you're drunk, my lad.

CYCLOPS
What say you, Silenus? Should I stay, do you think?

SILENUS
I do. You don't want to share your drink.

CYCLOPS
It's pleasant to sleep in the sweet long grass.   570

SILENUS
And sip wine in the sunshine, and let the world pass.
So down with you, come! Stretch your legs, never mind.

(*He quietly takes possession of the bowl.*)

CYCLOPS
Here, why are you hiding the bowl behind?

SILENUS
For fear it's turned over.

CYCLOPS
                    You're trying to wheedle
A sly drink or two. Set it back in the middle.
Now, stranger, I'm anxious your name to learn.

ODYSSEUS
I'm No-one. Have you nothing to give in return?

CYCLOPS
I'll not eat you—till I've eaten all the rest.

SILENUS
What a generous gift to give your guest. (*he drinks*)

CYCLOPS
Here, what are you doing, drinking on the sly?   580

SILENUS
The wine kissed my lips, so handsome am I.

CYCLOPS
I'll teach you to love wine, when it doesn't love you.

SILENUS
It says I'm so handsome it loves me true.

CYCLOPS
Pour me a cup, and give it to me.

SILENUS
Is the mixture right? Just let me see. (*he drinks*)

CYCLOPS
You'll be my ruin! Give it here, make haste!

SILENUS
Not till I wreathe you, and take a taste. (*drinks*)

CYCLOPS
Thieving swine!

SILENUS
　　　　　　No, pleasing wine, you should say.
First I'll wipe your nose, and then drink away. (*drinks*)

CYCLOPS
My mouth and whiskers are clean enough for me.　　　　　590

SILENUS
Now lie back on your elbows, gracefully,
And drink it down as you see me do—(*drinks*)
Or rather, as you don't.

CYCLOPS
　　　　　　　That's enough from you!
Here, what are you doing?

SILENUS
　　　　　　　　I've drunk it! O bliss!

CYCLOPS
Stranger, you shall serve me. Catch hold of this.

ODYSSEUS
It knows my hand. Now let's try it.

CYCLOPS
Fill her up.

ODYSSEUS
    I will, if you'll only be quiet.

CYCLOPS
That's asking a lot, when I'm full to the top.

ODYSSEUS
Now take it and drink it, and don't leave a drop.
You must only stop when there's no more wine.   600

CYCLOPS
What a wonderful tree it must be, this vine.

ODYSSEUS
If you fill yourself full on top of a feast
Till your thirst is gone, it will put you to sleep;
If you leave but a little, it leaves you dry.

CYCLOPS
Oh,
I could drown in this drink, it is deep in delight.
I see heaven sink, or so it seems,
To the land below; and aloft I see
High Zeus on his throne, and the heavenly throng
Of gods all together. The Graces beckon me,
But I'll not kiss them; Ganymedes here   610
Will satisfy me, by the Graces I swear it.

SILENUS (*apprehensively*)
Am I to play Ganymedes to your Zeus?

CYCLOPS
You are; I shall take you away from the Trojans.

SILENUS
Help, boys, or your father will lose his virtue.

CYCLOPS
I'm drunk; don't fight, I'm not going to hurt you.

SILENUS

Oh, now I shall drink the bitter dregs!

(*The* CYCLOPS *rushes into the cave with* SILENUS.)

ODYSSEUS

Come, Bacchus' boys, brave lads, be doing;
Our foe is inside; he will soon be asleep
Spewing foul flesh from his shameless stomach.
The stake sits smoking there inside   620
And nothing is undone but the deed itself,
To burn out his eye. Be men, I beseech you!

CHORUS

Our hearts will be flint-hard, hard as adamant.
But step inside, before our sire comes to grief.
We are here behind to help you, my lord.

ODYSSEUS

Hephaestus, thou that feedest Etna's fires,
Burn out the bright eye of this beast your neighbor
And rid this realm of thy rival for ever.
And Sleep, sweet nursling of somber Night,
Bring thy power to bear on this godless brute   630
Lest Odysseus be undone, and the mighty deeds
That he wrought in the wars of Troy be wasted
By a monster unmindful of god or man.
Else must we agree that chance is our god,
The greatest of gods, that governs all others.

(*Exit* ODYSSEUS *to the cave.*)

CHORUS

From his throat shall by and by
Come a strange and dreadful cry
As the stake burns out the eye
Of him who fed on strangers.
Bacchus master, be my guide,   640
Stand to help me at my side,
Crush the monster in his pride

And keep me out of dangers.

In the fire the trusty tree
Smoulders hot and waits for me.
Bacchus, Bacchus, hear my plea
And save me from disaster.
May the madman see no more,
May he sup on sorrow sore,
So I leave this lonely shore   650
And serve my merry master.

(*Enter* ODYSSEUS.)

ODYSSEUS
Have done with your howling in heaven's name!
Lock your lips up tight; I'll not let you breathe
Or wink or whisper to awaken him
And spoil our design, till the stake has pierced
The Cyclops' eye, and stolen his sight.

CHORUS
We shall take a big bite of air, and be quiet.

ODYSSEUS
Now hurry inside, set your hands to the stake.
Come, be busy; it is burning bright.

CHORUS (*edging away*)   660
Will it please you, appoint who shall take first place
At the stake to scorch out the Cyclops' eye,
So the luck may alight on all alike?

SOME OF THE CHORUS
I am too far from the door, I fear,
To sear out his eye from where I stand.

OTHERS
Alas, my leg has gone lame this minute.

OTHERS
I suffered the same; as I stood here
I twisted my ankle, I cannot tell how.

ODYSSEUS
What, sprained standing still?

OTHERS
                                        A sudden wind
Blew soot in our eyes, and we cannot see.

ODYSSEUS
You are cowards all, no counting on you.   670

CHORUS
You call us cowards, because we fear
To have our backs beaten black and blue
And would rather our teeth remained in our mouths?
But I know a fine song that Orpheus made
That will set the stake spinning by itself
And snatch from its socket the earth-child's eye.

ODYSSEUS
I knew all along you were of this nature
And know better now. I needs must turn
To my faithful friends. If you fear to help
Then sing us a chanty at least, to assure us   680
You wish us well, that we may work with good heart.

CHORUS
So shall we do, gallant Ithacan stranger,
Sing you a song as your stake spins about.
Ours is the cheering, and yours is the danger,
See if our chanty will tumble it out!
Heave ho, my hearties, heave harder and stronger,
Singe his great eyebrows and make the beast roar;
Blind him and burn him and let him no longer
Shepherd his sheep on our mountainous shore.

(A *roar is heard inside.*)

Turn it and twist it and take it out,   690
For fear in his frenzy he catch you a clout!

(*Enter the* CYCLOPS, *blind, his face running with blood.*)

CYCLOPS
They have burnt out my eye, these sailor men!

CHORUS
That's a good song, Cyclops; sing it again!

CYCLOPS
Alas, they have mocked me and made me blind.
But you cannot escape this cave of mine,
Little men, to laugh at me; I'll not allow you
Go past the gate, but guard it with my hands.

CHORUS
Why shout so, Cyclops?

CYCLOPS
                              I all but died.

CHORUS
Why, you look dreadful.

CYCLOPS
                              And wretched beside.

CHORUS
Were you so full of wine that you fell in the flames?   700

CYCLOPS
No-one destroyed me.

CHORUS
                              Then who's to blame?

CYCLOPS
No-one blinded me.

CHORUS
                              Then how are you blind?

CYCLOPS
Oh, I could give you—

CHORUS
                              If you'd be so kind,
How could no-one blind you? What do you mean?

CYCLOPS
You mock me; where's No-one?

CHORUS
                              Nowhere to be seen.

CYCLOPS
The wanderer has killed me, if you would know well,
May he ever be damned, who drenched me with drink.

CHORUS
Drink is a danger, and devilish tricky.

CYCLOPS
Have they slipped out, or did they stay inside?

CHORUS
They are standing silent on that shelf of rock.		710

CYCLOPS
On what hand?

CHORUS
                    On your right.

CYCLOPS
Come, are they in sight?

CHORUS
                              There, by the cliff face.

(*As the* CYCLOPS *lunges in one direction, the sailors slip by him on the other side.*)

CYCLOPS
Disgrace on disgrace! I've banged my head.

CHORUS
And the sailors have fled.

CYCLOPS
Over here, did you say?

CHORUS
                    No, the other way.
To your left, turn round. They've gone to ground.

(*As he turns, more men slip past him.*)

CYCLOPS
You laugh at my misery, mock at my woes.

CHORUS
No, no! There's No-one, in front of your nose!

CYCLOPS
Wretch, where are you?

ODYSSEUS
                              Away from harm,
Defending Odysseus' body from danger.   720

CYCLOPS
You have changed your name for a name I dread.

ODYSSEUS
My name is Odysseus, as my father called me.
Did you think you could eat us and escape scot-free?
Much good did it do us to drag Troy down
If you feasted on my friends, and I forgave you.

CYCLOPS
As the prophets promised, it has come to pass,
That I should be blinded by you and your band
On your travels from Troy. This too they foretold,
That to pay for my pain you should pine long years
Adrift on the deep, before your journey is done.   730

ODYSSEUS
Go perish, I pray you; the prophecy's complete.
Come, friends, to the coast, and cast off our keel
To Sicily's sea, and my ancestral home.

CYCLOPS
No, rogue, for I'll wrench this rock from its seat
And cast it to crush you, crew and all.
I shall mount this cliff, though I cannot see,
And climb through the corridors of my cave!

(The CYCLOPS *goes into his cave, as* ODYSSEUS *and his men, with the chorus following, exit to a song of triumph.)*

CHORUS
We'll sail with King Odysseus
From Etna's lonely shore
And find our old lord Bacchus   740
And serve him evermore!

NOTES

4 *Hera's fury* Silenus touches briefly on several of the traditional Dionysus stories: the jealousy of Hera, who drove him
in a fit of temporary madness from the nymphs of Mount
Nysa in Thrace—the nymphs who had nursed him; the
celebrated battle between gods and giants for the possession
of the world; and the kidnapping of Dionysus by pirates,
whom he escaped by causing a vine to grow in the ship and
changing his captors into dolphins. The latter scene is one
of the most famous representations of Greek vase painting.

131 *Sisyphus* See note on *Medea* l. 380.

168 *Maron* The priest of Apollo, whose life Odysseus had
spared.

283 *by Poseidon your sire* Polyphemus was the son of the sea-
god. Silenus hopes to make his oath doubly impressive by
involving all the marine deities he can think of.

295 *Rhadamanthus* Brother of King Minos of Crete; because
of the justice he had displayed throughout his life, he was
made a judge of the underworld.

320 *At our land's far limits* Sicily, in historical times the home
of some of the wealthiest Greek colonies, is regarded even in
this legendary setting as coming under Greek influence.

343 *I take no thought* . . . This speech has been regarded as an
example of Euripides' atheism; but he does no more than bor-
row from Homer.

512 *for I quit the cave* The nature of the Greek theatre requires that the action must be represented as taking place outside the cave, but the audience must still be kept informed
about what goes on inside. The plot is such that Euripides
cannot employ the traditional messenger. Thus Odysseus
must be brought out again, and an excuse must be found to
explain his presence. It is a weak one—we might well ask
why his companions could not have escaped in the same
way.

542 *Lover, leave your pacing* The satyrs draw a macabre
parallel between the Cyclops' approaching fate and a wedding

feast. By "bridal torches" they allude to the stake, by "blossoms red" the tongues of fire, or perhaps the Cyclops' blood.

577 *I'm No-one* Euripides passes over summarily the matter of Odysseus' feigned name, one of the most important incidents in Homer.

610 *Ganymedes* A beautiful Trojan boy stolen by Zeus to be his cup-bearer.

626 *Hephaestus* The blacksmith god, patron of fires and forges, and believed to have his workshops inside volcanoes.

731 *the prophecy's complete* Another instance of somewhat clumsy dramatic adaptation. In Homer the prophecy is fulfilled. Here Euripides has to get his chorus off the stage and finish the play neatly. He thus makes Odysseus reply, unnaturally, that the prophesied wanderings have already been completed!

The Frogs / ARISTOPHANES

INTRODUCTION

I. OLD COMEDY

THE Greek Old Comedy, of which Aristophanes is our sole extant representative, had been known from its beginnings for its freedom and lack of inhibition. It moved in the world of high fantasy. Its choruses could represent birds, animals, cities, or whatever the poet pleased; real and fictional characters stood side by side. The humor of Old Comedy was similarly eclectic. The Athenian audience was drawn from all ranks of society, from highbrows and lowbrows, poets, pedants and plebs, the respectable bourgeoisie and the rabble of the city streets. If the comic poet wished to please, and to stand a fair chance of winning the prize, he had to appeal equally to all levels of taste and intelligence. Tragedy, though popular, was by no means everyman's entertainment, but comedy aimed to please all. Thus Old Comedy runs the gamut of humor, from political satire to obscene jesting, from literary parody at its most subtle to the fool's bladder and the custard pie. Not the least interesting feature of Aristophanes' work is the way he contrives to keep all these balls in the air at the same time, and never leaves any section of his audience neglected for too long. He is not one to pander to the intellectuals. Clever wit there is in plenty, but never for too long at a time. As soon as there is danger of the coarser elements in the audience becoming restive, in comes some uproarious buffoonery, some ready obscenity to set the groundlings laughing again. This all-embracing concept of humor sometimes makes modern audiences uneasy. Our ideas of theatre have become more restricted, and we prefer our plays neatly categorized. We like to watch high comedy or low comedy, satire or farce, but not all at the same time. Aristophanes' audience would have had little sympathy with such an attitude.

Old Comedy in its purest form took its targets where it pleased. It was no respecter of persons. The leader of the state was as liable to attack as the humblest private citizen. Comedy, like tragedy, was expected to be functional, to prove itself serviceable to the state (a further difference between ancient comedy and modern); and it could amply justify itself by providing a safety valve for popular emotions, by pointing the finger of scorn at excess and pretentiousness wherever they were to be found—in politics, in the arts, in private life. Just so, the Emperors of Byzantium were to give free rein to licensed buffoons; just so did the medieval jester enjoy a privileged position in his royal master's court.

But such free criticism, delivered at the city's most public gathering, could only be possible when the democracy felt itself secure. Criticism from within can only be tolerated when there is no pressure from without. The nearest, perhaps the only, equivalents to Old Comedy in the modern theatre are the works of Gilbert and Sullivan; and it is significant that these biting satires on the most sacred British institutions were composed at a period when the British economy was at its most secure. More precarious governments could not risk such outspoken criticism. As the Peloponnesian War dragged on and the hopes of Athens dwindled, as the old democracy gave way to demagogy and murmurs of revolution, Old Comedy gradually lost its trenchant force. It was no longer safe to abuse the mighty. Aristophanes was forced to lower his sights to less dangerous targets and turn from political to social and literary satire.

It is to this period of his work that *The Frogs* belongs. Written in 405 B.C., in the closing years of the war, it was performed in an Athens that had already suffered many grave reverses. The war and current politics have their place in the play; but there is nothing like the unremitting attack on leading statesmen and their politics that characterizes *The Knights* and *The Acharnians*. Aristophanes has turned his attention to literary matters.

The current state of the drama was one which might well claim a dramatic poet's attention. In the course of a year the tragic stage had lost its two most brilliant figures. Euripides, though the younger man, died first—not in Athens, but as an exile in the court of a friendly king, where the hostility of his own people, exacerbated by defeat, had sent him. Sophocles, it is said, led out his chorus in mourning for his fellow tragedian when the death was known, and himself died soon afterwards, leaving his last play, *Oedipus at Colonus*, to be performed posthumously. The theatre was diminished by their passing; and in half-comic, half-serious recognition of this, Aristophanes invents a plot in which Dionysus, God of the Theatre, undertakes a pilgrimage to the Underworld to resurrect Euripides. In the second half of the play this divine adventure is expanded into a scintillating commentary on the ways of drama and dramatists.

Old Comedy had never been a model of plot-construction. The immediate joke was the important thing, and this condones all manner of digressions and irrelevancies. Aristophanes' early plays are little more than a series of skits loosely connected by a central character or theme. This is something else which tends to offend modern critics of the purer sort; but we would be wrong to apply modern notions of consistency to this most uninhibited of drama-forms, or complain because the plays do not fit our mold. The chief virtue of Old Comedy was its freedom, its power to jump from one topic to another, to add or shed characters as the dramatist's whim suggested. In the latter stages of Aristophanes' career the increasing limitations of material tended to induce, by way of compensation, a tighter plot-structure (compare, for example, *The Acharnians*, 425 B.C., with *Lysistrata*, 411 B.C.; the latter is much nearer modern ideas of what a comedy should be), but *The Frogs* still leaves much to be desired according to modern standards of dramatic tidiness. Dionysus begins with the avowed intention of recovering Euripides, and this carries us through the picaresque adventures of the first half of the play. Then there occurs a sudden *volte-face*. We are introduced, almost without warning, to a tragic competition between Aeschylus, Grand Old Man of the Greek theatre and now dead for a generation, and Euripides, to decide which is the better poet. Dionysus awards the prize to Aeschylus and takes him back to the upper world. Why the change of plan? We might suggest, perhaps, that in the first half of the play Aristophanes has exhausted all possible variations on the journey-to-the-underworld theme. If he were simply to find Euripides and bring him back the play might become repetitive. (This danger is illustrated by *The Birds*, whose situation does not allow of sufficient variation, so that Aristophanes tends to repeat his effects.) He might, alternatively, illustrate Euripides' escape by a series of tragic parodies; but he has already used a similar device in *Thesmophoriazousae*. And so he hits on the idea of expanding his original conception into a comic examination of the problems of tragedy, focusing upon its two most antagonistic representatives.

Why does Sophocles not figure more prominently in the play? There are only a couple of references to him. Probably much had been written before Sophocles died, and further incorporation would have meant too extensive a revision at a late stage in the work. Also, given that Aristophanes wishes to contrast two styles of playwriting, Aeschylus and Euripides make a much more effective contrast than would either one of them with Sophocles, who represents a transitional stage between the two. And so Sophocles, though present in spirit, remains an off-stage figure. It is between Aeschylus and Euripides, between the old drama and the new, that the battle is fought out.

What was Aristophanes' opinion of the two dramatists? How far does the trial reveal his own tastes? Does the awarding of the prize to Aeschylus indicate his own preference? Much has been written on the subject; but it is perhaps un-

fair to press the question too hard. We must remember that
Aristophanes was first and foremost a comedian, and not a
literary critic. His main function is to make people laugh.
We must beware of taking everything he says too seriously.
Aristophanes has suffered too much from the heavy-handed,
pedantic sort of modern criticism that would find deep meaning in every line. His *general* remarks about tragedy are well
worth attention. Notice how both Aeschylus and Euripides
are made to agree on the function of tragedy—it should not
merely entertain but instruct, and seek the well-being of the
state through a serious examination of moral problems. With
this any Greek would have agreed. Where the tragedians
differ is in their application of this principle. Aeschylus insists that tragedy should shun the sordid and commonplace,
and concentrate on instilling high ideals and patriotic fervor;
Euripides, that it should teach men how to think for themselves, show life as it really is, present men with provocative
questions and not pretend to know all the answers. But
Aristophanes typically exaggerates both sides of the question.
Aeschylus is inflated into a Kiplingesque figure with Boy
Scout morals. Euripides becomes a sensationalist, a restless
innovator for innovation's sake. What did Aristophanes
really think of Euripides? He burlesques him cruelly in three
plays. In many ways the two had much in common. Both
delighted in ridiculing pretensions, though Euripides' attacks were written with a more savage pen. This innate
sympathy gives the comedian a better appreciation of the
tragedian's weaknesses, and he turns his intimate knowledge
of Euripides' work to comic advantage. As a comic poet he
had to find something to be funny about, and, more particularly, something which would be familiar to as many
segments of his audience as possible. Eccentricity and un-
orthodoxy were his obvious targets; in his private life and in
his public career Euripides qualified on both counts. In *The
Acharnians* Aristophanes satirizes his innovations in staging

and costuming, in *Thesmophoriazousae* his new style of melodramatic tragedy. In *The Frogs* he is concerned both with content and style—with Euripides' theories of what tragedy should consist of, and his innovations in music and metre.

We cannot expect a satirist to be entirely fair, or to contain his attacks within reasonable bounds. Some of the things he says about Euripides are mere nonsense. The trial itself is a farce; the final questions are not concerned with poetry at all, but with politics. Aeschylus is satirized equally unmercifully, and Euripides is allowed to make some good points. But, at least so far as any theory of poetry is concerned, the verdict is as irrelevant as much of the criticism. Dionysus' indecision probably represents Aristophanes' own; in each there was much to admire and something to condemn.

2. THE POLITICAL BACKGROUND

WHAT of the other elements in the play? Though primarily a literary comedy, *The Frogs* could not wholly escape the comedian's responsibility for keeping a watchful eye on current affairs. The war has its place, though in the background. We hear several times of the battle of Arginousae, fought in the previous year. This isolated victory had unfortunate repercussions that well illustrate the essential volatility of the Athenian temperament. The Athenian ships had beaten the Spartans, but had suffered some losses. In the excitement of battle the Athenian generals had not stopped to collect the bodies of their fellows and give them proper burial. At home this oversight was exaggerated into an affront to religious sentiment; the generals were formally accused, and those who were foolish enough to return to Athens were punished. But in his political comments Aristophanes was concerned not so much with specific instances as with the fickleness of the Athenians, and their propensity to turn on their own saviors, which the Arginousae incident illustrates. The democracy was falling apart, and Athens was the prey of squabbling factions that contributed more to the eventual disaster than did any maneuvers of the Spartans. In *The Frogs* Aristophanes preaches the lesson of tolerance and forgiveness. Let Athens recognize her true friends; let her mitigate the resentment of the past, abandon her animosity and ask those who had stood by her once to come to her aid again. Aristophanes focuses on the case of Alcibiades, Golden Boy of the late fifth century, the outstanding example of a patriot and hero who had been alienated by the pettiness of his fellow-citizens. His message came too late to be effective, though many in the audience must have recognized its force, and sympathized. Athens was growing weary of war, and weary of squabbling. It may well have been Aristophanes' appeal for a new start that gave the play its first prize, and the unusual honor of a second performance.

3. THE TITLE

ONE last question: why is the play called *The Frogs* at all? Why should Aristophanes have named his comedy not after the main chorus of Initiates, as was customary, but after the supplementary chorus which appears in only one brief scene? There are several possible explanations. Many comedies had animal choruses—their use goes back to the earliest origins of this drama-form, in fertility rites and rustic festivals—and he may well have wished to continue the tradition. It is also possible that he wanted to avoid confusion with another comedy in the same festival. Phrynichus offered *The Muses* (*Musai*), which won second prize; perhaps *The Initiated* (*Mustoi*) would have sounded too similar. And, in the last analysis, we should not object that Aristophanes has chosen to name his play after its most brilliant single episode. For sheer wit and metrical inventiveness the frog chorus deserves a high place among the poet's compositions;

and its haunting, repetitive refrain of "Brekekekex koax koax" is known to many who have never consciously heard a Greek comedy in their lives.

4. THE CHARACTERS

IN the other characters of the play Aristophanes shows his customary fertility of invention, Dionysus, the central figure, is one of his most inspired creations. This god was a late addition to the Greek pantheon. His worship originated in Asia Minor, and even after his adoption by the Greeks he retained traces of Oriental softness and luxury, not to say cruelty. These qualities could inspire a terrifying portrait such as Euripides draws of him in *The Bacchae*; in *The Frogs* Aristophanes distorts and exaggerates, producing a Dionysus who is a caricature of the weak, over-cultured and effeminate intellectual. The fact that two such dissimilar portraits of a major deity could be produced within a few years testifies equally to the freedom of the Greek theatre and the freedom of Greek religion.

In considering Dionysus, and any other character in Greek comedy, we must beware of applying modern conceptions of dramatic characterization to this ancient form. As in plot, so in characterization: logic and consistency are sacrificed to the immediate comic situation. At the beginning of his journey Dionysus displays admirable firmness of mind; once he is in the Underworld, it is obviously more humorous to represent him as a coward, and so he becomes one. The God of Tragedy who is such a master of critical jargon in the first half of the play lapses into sophomoric imbecility in the second. The aesthete who shudders at his servant's coarseness has some of the best vulgarities in the play. But these things are not important. This type of comedy lives for the moment, and we are never disturbed by any sense of incongruity.

As Don Quixote needs his Sancho Panza, as Mr. Pickwick needs his Sam Weller, as Bud Abbott needs his Lou Costello, so Dionysus needs his Xanthias. The slave is a perfect foil to his master. Comedy deals largely in the inversion of the norm, and the slave who bullies his master is one of the oldest comic figures in the world. Xanthias represents a type familiar on the Athenian comic stage. He is shrewd and resourceful; he has a knack for getting himself out of awkward situations and for getting his master into them. Aristophanes occasionally boasted that he was above low comedy. He could certainly inject new life into the stock figures; but his characterization of Xanthias shows that he was equally at home with the good old jokes, and could use them as skillfully as anyone else.

Heracles is another stock figure of the comic stage. He was customarily represented as a glutton and buffoon, the prototype of the athlete with muscles of iron and a brain of solid ivory. Apart from his particular function in the present plot (the disguise motif) his bovine muscularity shows up Dionysus' antithetical qualities in even stronger relief.

In portraying the workings of the Underworld Aristophanes could draw upon an already highly picturesque eschatology. Charon with his boat is a figure familiar in Greek mythology; he survives as Charondas, a figure of death, in modern Greek folklore. Aeacus is another familiar figure, who has been demoted for comic purposes. In mythology he was one of the Judges of the Dead, a powerful personage in the Underworld. Here, like St. Peter in Christian humor, he is assigned the lowly position of doorkeeper. Pluto, Lord of the Dead, makes only a brief appearance, and his queen Persephone is introduced only by name. Once Dionysus has reached his destination the setting is largely forgotten and interest is centered on the tragic poets. Among these mythological figures, Aristophanes interweaves with sublime and calculated incongruity figures from everyday life, like the two rapacious tavernkeepers who might have walked straight off any ancient, or modern, Greek street. Their normality emphasizes by contrast the play's rich fantasy.

The main chorus of the comedy is composed of Initiates of the Eleusinian Mysteries. This cult was devoted to the worship of Demeter, Goddess of Growing Things, and her daughter Persephone, who had been abducted by Pluto to be his queen but, by decree of the gods, returned to earth to live with her mother for six months in every year. This was in origin a nature myth—Persephone's coming and going symbolize summer and winter—but in the later stages of Greek religion came to mean much more than this. As the traditional religion began to lose its force, the Greeks turned more and more to mystery cults which extended some hope of personal immortality and of rewards in the next life for suffering endured in this. The Persephone story easily adapted itself to such doctrines, and her shrine at Eleusis, a few miles from Athens, became an important center. Every year a procession set out from Athens to Eleusis along the Sacred Way, in an atmosphere of revelry and holiday making. Dionysus had infiltrated himself into this rite, as he had into many others, and it is under his name of Iacchus that we find him invoked here. Aristophanes reproduces the mood of this procession and plays on the resurrection-revival theme to produce a chorus equally at home in this world and the next.

5. THE TRANSLATION

THIS is a version designed for acting, and as such imposes special limitations on the translator. A stage performance, if it is to succeed, must be self-explanatory and immediately intelligible. There is no place for footnotes in the theatre. The audience cannot take time out to look up obscure references; and in any case, nothing kills a joke so surely as explanation. This means that the most conscientious translator must resign himself to the impossibility of reproducing many of the jokes as written. Aristophanes relies to a large extent on topicality—on introducing references to characters, events and places intimately familiar to the Athenian audience of his time. Such jokes now fall completely flat. Even before the most learned audience in the world, topicality ceases to be funny when it is no longer topical. There seem to be two ways of dealing with this problem. One, often adopted, is to replace the ancient topicalities by modern ones. Well done, this can be brilliantly effective, but is itself limited. First we have to cope with the law of libel, unknown to Aristophanes. Second, we live in a larger world. It is impossible to parallel every one of Aristophanes' references with a topicality equally pungent in New York, Dallas, Milwaukee and San Francisco, let alone London or Toronto. The other method, and the one adopted here, is to strike out the proper names, to reproduce the content rather than the letter of the joke and generalize where Aristophanes particularizes. The present version concentrates on humor rather than pedantry, even at the risk of departing from the original text. Notes have been included, for the sake of completeness, to supply something of a historical background; but if the jokes need the notes to explain them, they have failed. The aim has been to provide a version which, while remaining as close as possible to Aristophanes' original intentions, can be performed as comedy before any reasonably intelligent theatre audience. Each line has been subjected to the acid test of public performance; and the author wishes to express his thanks to the cast of the first production of this translation, in the theatre of the State University of Iowa in January, 1960, for the numerous improvements and modifications which they suggested.

The Frogs is a comedy on a literary theme, and the original text is replete with allusions to Greek literature— sometimes long quotations, sometimes a word or a phrase. Some of these, though by no means all, have been paralleled here by corresponding allusions to English literature; and the reader must not be surprised to discover echoes of Marlowe, Shakespeare, Burns and Ogden Nash. If such random borrowing seems irreverent, this translation will have conveyed at least one of the characteristics of Greek Old Comedy.

CHARACTERS

DIONYSUS   God of Tragedy
XANTHIAS   his slave
HERACLES   a demigod
A CORPSE
CHARON   ferryman of the dead
CHORUS OF FROGS
CHORUS OF INITIATES
AEACUS   doorkeeper of the Underworld
SERVANT   of the Queen of the Dead
FIRST TAVERNKEEPER
SECOND TAVERNKEEPER
EURIPIDES
AESCHYLUS } rival tragedians
PLUTO   King of the Dead

Bier-bearers, servants of Aeacus, the Muse of Euripides.

(The play begins in front of the house of HERACLES *in Athens. Enter* DIONYSUS *and* XANTHIAS, *the former grotesquely dressed in a lionskin—traditional costume of* HERACLES—*over elaborate tragic robes, the latter riding a donkey and loaded down with baggage which he carries on a porter's pole across his shoulders.* XANTHIAS *takes cognizance of the audience, and at once breaks into his familiar low comedy act.)*

XANTHIAS
Well master, shall I go into the old routine
That always has 'em rolling in the aisles?

DIONYSUS
Whatever you like, except "I've sprung a leak."
You can cut that out. It's *nauseating.*

XANTHIAS
Nothing sophisticated?

DIONYSUS
                         Not "Oh boy, I'm loaded."

XANTHIAS
Can't I say *anything* funny?

DIONYSUS
                         Be my guest.
But you can leave out that one—

XANTHIAS
                         What one?

DIONYSUS
The one where you shift your pole across your shoulders
And say "I wish I knew what I could do with this."

XANTHIAS
What about this? "I've got such a load on board,   10
Unless someone relieves me, I'll have to relieve myself."

DIONYSUS
No thanks! When I want my stomach turned I'll ask you.

XANTHIAS

Then what's the point of carrying all these props
If I can't prop up the act with them, like the porters
In everybody else's comedies?

DIONYSUS

Just you dare! Whenever I go to a show
And see those tired old gags, I come away
A year or more older than when I went in.

XANTHIAS

Well, poor old neck of mine, I'm sorry for you.
You're loaded, and you can't make jokes about it.   20

DIONYSUS

Just listen to him talking back at me,
When I, Dionysus, one hundred proof,
Struggle along on foot, and have him carried
So that he shouldn't lift weights and tire himself!

XANTHIAS

I'm lifting things!

DIONYSUS

                    You're not, you've got a lift!

XANTHIAS

I'm lifting these!

DIONYSUS

                    How?

XANTHIAS

                    With a deal of trouble.

DIONYSUS

But you're not lifting them, the donkey is!

XANTHIAS

No, not what I've got here he isn't, I am.

DIONYSUS

How can you be when you've got a lift yourself?

XANTHIAS

Don't ask me. (*getting his favorite joke in at last*) I wish I knew
   what I could do with this!   30

DIONYSUS

Well, if you say the donkey isn't helping
Take turns and let the donkey have a ride.

XANTHIAS

Good grief! Why didn't I go and join the navy?
Then I could tell you to go and kick yourself.

DIONYSUS

Get down, you bum. Here we are at the door,
My first port of call. (*knocks*)
                          Hey! Anyone at home?

(*Enter* HERACLES. *He too wears a lionskin, and carries a club—
though with more grace than the effeminate* DIONYSUS.)

HERACLES

Who's knocking at my door? He's got a kick
Like a mule, whoever he is. (*unable to believe his eyes*) Lan'sakes,
   whatever's this? (*he roars with laughter*)

DIONYSUS
Xanthias!

XANTHIAS
     What?

DIONYSUS
               Didn't you notice?

XANTHIAS
                        What?

DIONYSUS
How scared he was.

XANTHIAS
           Yes, scared he was going nuts.   40

HERACLES

So help me, I can't keep myself from laughing.
I'm biting my lips but it makes no difference.

DIONYSUS (*offended*)

Here, wonder-boy, I want to ask you something.

HERACLES

No, this is too much! I'm hysterical!
(*Pointing at* DIONYSUS' *theatrical costume and footwear*.)
Look at the lionskin on the yellow tunic!
What's the idea? How does the club go together
With the old soft shoe? Where on earth are you off to?

DIONYSUS

I joined the marines.

HERACLES

See any action?

DIONYSUS

Yes, and sank
Some enemy ships, at least a dozen of them.

HERACLES

You did?

DIONYSUS

You bet.

XANTHIAS (*aside*)

And then they woke me up.   50

DIONYSUS

And one day as I sat on the foredeck, reading
That play by Euripides, "The Perils of Andromeda,"
I was suddenly smitten by a great desire.

HERACLES

Desire? How big?

DIONYSUS

A mere nothing! Six feet six in its socks.

HERACLES (*leering*)
Who was the lady?

DIONYSUS (*being patient with this barbarian*)
It wasn't for a lady.

HERACLES
Who was the boy then?

DIONYSUS
                    No, nothing like that!

HERACLES
A man?

DIONYSUS
        Oh really!

HERACLES
                    Some of those officers . . .

DIONYSUS
Don't laugh at me, brother. I'm in a bad way.
This desire is really burning me up.

HERACLES
Come on, tell brother.

DIONYSUS
                    I don't know how to put it   60
In a way you'd understand. Let's try an example.
Have you ever had a mad desire for soup?

HERACLES (*immediately roused*)
Soup! I should say so! Yes, a million times!

DIONYSUS
Now shall I give it you straight? Or would you like
Another example?

HERACLES
                Not about soup.
You can't tell me anything about soup.

DIONYSUS
Such is the passion gnawing at my heart
For Euripides.

HERACLES
                    Euripides?
(It gradually sinks in.)
                                    He's dead!

DIONYSUS
I'm going to fetch him. No-one will put me off.

HERACLES
Down to the Underworld?

DIONYSUS
                                    Deeper if I have to.   70

HERACLES
But what are you after?

DIONYSUS
                    An able poet.
For some are gone; there's worse remains behind.

HERACLES
Why, what about the son of Sophocles?

DIONYSUS
Yes, he's the only good thing left, if we can count him.
I really don't know what to make of him.

HERACLES
But if you have to resurrect somebody
Why not take Sophocles before Euripides?

DIONYSUS
Not till I've seen the son without his father
On his own, and tried the metal of his verses.
Besides, Euripides was game for anything.   80
He'd take the risk and run away with me.
But Sophocles will be happy where he is,
Just as he was on earth.

HERACLES
What about Agathon?

DIONYSUS
          Gone off and left me.
A splendid poet, and his friends will miss him.

HERACLES
Gone where, poor fellow?

DIONYSUS
          The Happy Hunting Ground.

HERACLES
And Xenocles?

DIONYSUS
        Oh, Xenocles be damned!

HERACLES
Pythangelus?

XANTHIAS
        Nobody mentions me
Although my shoulder's nearly worn away.

HERACLES
But aren't there other artsy-craftsy kids,
Ten thousand of 'em, writing tragedies   90
More chatty than Euripides by miles?

DIONYSUS
Deadwood the lot of them, so much hot air,
Performing parrots prostituting art!
They open, drop their filth on Tragedy
And then you never hear of them again.
You'll never find a poet alive today
Who's creative, who writes high-class dialogue.

HERACLES
What do you mean, creative?

DIONYSUS
           Somebody
Who conjures up some scintillating phrase

Like "God's log cabin in the skies," "Time marches on,"
Or "Conscience that will not commit itself
While tongue is free to practice perjury."

HERACLES
You like that sort of thing?

DIONYSUS

It really sends me.

HERACLES
You mean it's a lot of humbug.

DIONYSUS
My mind's my business! You can mind your own!

HERACLES
What's more, it's a pack of downright wicked nonsense.

DIONYSUS
Your taste is in your mouth!

XANTHIAS

Not a word about me!

DIONYSUS
Now the reason why I came here in this costume,
Disguised as you, is this; I want you to tell me
The friends who put you up, when you went to Hades   110
To steal its watchdog, just in case I need them.
Tell me your hosts, the harbors, bakeries,
Brothels, pull-ins, short cuts, fountains, highways,
The towns, the dinner-parties and hotels which had
The fewest bugs.

XANTHIAS

And not a word about me.

HERACLES
You wouldn't dare! You'd really risk it? You?

DIONYSUS
Now that's enough of that. Just let me know
The most direct route to the Underworld

And don't give one that's too hot or too cold.

HERACLES
Which one shall I tell you first, now, eh?   120
There's one that goes by way of rope and drop,
By hanging yourself.

DIONYSUS
                    Oh stop, you're taking my breath away.

HERACLES
Or a quick one, straight, not even on the rocks—
In a mortar.

DIONYSUS
          You mean by hemlock?

HERACLES
That's it.

DIONYSUS
          No, that's a cold and wintry way.
It makes you a bit chilly round the ankles.

HERACLES
Do you want a fast route, downhill all the way?

DIONYSUS
Yes, that's for me. I've always hated walking.

HERACLES
Then take a stroll to the Potters' Quarter—

DIONYSUS
                                   Then what?

HERACLES
Climb to the top of the high tower—

DIONYSUS
                              What to do?   130

HERACLES
And when you hear the spectators shout "They're off,"
Then off you go.

DIONYSUS

        Go off? Go where?

HERACLES

Why, over the edge.

DIONYSUS

        No thank you very much.
I'd spoil these two brain puddings. No, not that way.

HERACLES

How will you go then?

DIONYSUS

        The way you went before.

HERACLES

It's a long voyage. The first thing you come to
Is a great lake, bottomless.

DIONYSUS

        How do I get over?

HERACLES

An old salt will ferry you across
In a cockleshell, this size, and charge one dollar.   140

DIONYSUS

Almighty dollar! How you get around!
What are they doing with dollars in Hell?

HERACLES

Where there are politicians, there must be money.
After that you'll see snakes and wild beasts, millions of 'em,
Terrifying.

DIONYSUS

        Don't keep trying to scare me.
You'll never put me off.

HERACLES

        Then a great big swamp
And ever-flowing filth, and wallowing in it

Anyone who's ever wronged a guest,
Beaten his mother, punched father on the jaw
Or sworn an oath and then gone back on it   150
Or copied speeches out of third-rate plays.

DIONYSUS (*to the audience*)
And I should hope to see there anyone
Who's learned the rock-and-roll from what's-his-name!

HERACLES
And then a breath of flutes will greet your ears
And you'll see a light as radiant as here
And myrtle groves, and blessed companies
Of men and women, dancing, clapping hands. . . .

DIONYSUS
And who might they be?

HERACLES
The Initiated!

XANTHIAS
And I'm the donkey at the Mysteries!
I'm not going to carry these things a minute longer.   160

HERACLES
They'll tell you everything you need to know.
They have their houses just beside the road
At Pluto's door. Well, goodbye brother mine.
Have a good trip.

DIONYSUS
And the best of health to you!

(*Exit* HERACLES. DIONYSUS *turns to* XANTHIAS.)

Here you, pick up the bags again!

XANTHIAS
I haven't put them down yet!

DIONYSUS
Be quick.

XANTHIAS

Please master, can't you hail a passing corpse?
Someone who's going the same way that we are?

DIONYSUS

Suppose I can't find anybody?

XANTHIAS

I'll do it.

DIONYSUS

Fair enough.

(*Enter* CORPSE *with* BEARERS.)

Here comes a funeral procession now.   170
Here you! Yes, you're the one I mean, the dead one.
Would you like to take a few bags down to Hades?

CORPSE

How many?

DIONYSUS

These here.

CORPSE

It'll cost five dollars.

DIONYSUS

That's highway robbery!

CORPSE

Bearers, on your way!

DIONYSUS

Here, wait a minute, can't we compromise?

CORPSE

Five dollars down, or you're wasting your breath.

DIONYSUS

Three fifty?

CORPSE

Over my living body!

(*Exeunt* CORPSE *and* BEARERS.)

DIONYSUS
Well, damn his insolence.

XANTHIAS
                    He'll suffer for it.
I'll take them.

DIONYSUS
                    Good lad, you're one of the best.
Let's go down to the ferry.   180

(*The scene changes to the River Styx. Enter* CHARON *in his boat.*)

CHARON
Heave ho, lay her alongside!

XANTHIAS
Whatever's this?

DIONYSUS
                    Well, heavens above, a lake!
The one he told us about! And there's a boat!

XANTHIAS
Ye gods and little fishes! Look, there's Charon!

DIONYSUS
Ahoy, ahoy, ahoy !

CHARON
Who's for the rest cure from work and worry,
Oblivion Valley, Rockcandy Mountain,
Who's going to the dogs, the vultures, the Cape of Bad Hope?

DIONYSUS
I am!

CHARON
 Hurry up, get in.

DIONYSUS
                    Where do you say you're going?
The vultures? Really?

CHARON
That's the place for you!   190
Come on, get in.

DIONYSUS (*embarking*)
Here, Xanthias!

CHARON
No slaves allowed,
Unless he's earned the Veterans' Bill of Rights.

XANTHIAS
I'm afraid I haven't. I had 4F vision.

CHARON
Then you can make the circuit on your feet.

XANTHIAS
Where shall I meet you?

CHARON
At the terminus
By Withering Heights.

DIONYSUS
You understand?

XANTHIAS
Too right I do.
I was born unlucky. There's a hoodoo on this trip.
(*Exit.*)

CHARON
Trim your oar. (DIONYSUS *takes him literally*)
Any other passengers? Hurry!
Here you, what do you think you're doing?

DIONYSUS
Me?
Obeying orders, trimming my oar.   200

CHARON
Would you be good enough to sit here, potbelly?

DIONYSUS
There.

CHARON
Now put out your arms and stretch.

DIONYSUS (*misunderstanding hopelessly*)
Like that?

CHARON
STOP MONKEYING ABOUT! Put your feet against the stretcher
And pull with a will.

DIONYSUS
And how do you expect a man like me,
Unskilled, unseaworthy, un-Salaminian,
To row?

CHARON
That's easy. You'll hear the most beautiful
Songs, as soon as you start rowing.

DIONYSUS
Whose songs?

CHARON
Wonderful swan-frog songs.

DIONYSUS
Then give the stroke.

CHARON
In, out! In, out! In, out!   210

(*As the boat begins to move off, a chorus of* FROGS *appears. They
sing and dance, setting a tempo that* DIONYSUS *has trouble in following.*)

FROGS
Brekekekex koax, brekekekex koax,
Brekekekex koax, koax!
Children of marsh and river,
Let's make sweet harmony together

And sing the melody that we used to sing
To Bacchus the son of Heaven's King!
As we sang in Athens at his yearly revels
When he came among us from the Asian shore
While the crowd of worshippers with sacred vessels
Went reeling drunk around his temple door.   220
Brekekekex koax, brekekekex koax,
Brekekekex koax, koax!

DIONYSUS
My bottom's sore—

    FROGS
                  Brekekekex koax

DIONYSUS
As if you cared—

    FROGS
                  Brekekekex koax

DIONYSUS
Goddam you all and your koax,
There's nothing inside you but koax!

    FROGS
    Yes indeed, that's so very true,
    But whatever has it to do with you?   230
    For horny-hoofed Pan on my reed-pipes plays
    And we are the Muses' protegés!

    For they are heaven's instrumentalists
    And reeds for their instruments require
    And so we grow them in our mud beneath the water and
    Apollo is delighted to use them for his lyre!

    Brekekekex koax, brekekekex koax,
    Brekekekex koax, koax.

    DIONYSUS (*desperately trying to row at a more reasonable
      speed*)
    I'm getting blisters where I sit,

My bottom is sweating away.   240
In just another little bit
It will arise and say—

FROGS
Brekekekex koax, brekekekex koax,
Brekekekex koax, koax!

DIONYSUS (*in extremis*)
Singing sisters, stop the music!

FROGS
We'll sing much louder, we will sing much more
Than we have ever sung before!
We'll sing if ever in high summer we
Swam among the rushes and the water lily,
Diving to the depths to dodge showery weather   250
With a splish splash gurgle from the bed of the river.

DIONYSUS
Brekekekex koax, I've got it now!

FROGS
Hey, we're in trouble!

DIONYSUS
So would I be if
Rowing brought on one of my attacks—

FROGS
Brekekekex koax, koax!

DIONYSUS
Sing away, it does not worry me.

FROGS
You won't be rid of us so easily.
We'll keep on singing till our larynx cracks—

DIONYSUS
Brekekekex koax, koax!   260
I'll never give you the victory.

FROGS
You'll never boast that you've beaten me.

DIONYSUS
I'll never be outdone by you,
Just listen and see what I can do!
I can sing all day if it's necessary
Till I've knocked the koax out of you!
Brekekekex koax, koax
I knew in the end I'd stop your koax!

(*Exeunt* FROGS.)

CHARON
Heave ho! Back water! Lay her alongside!
Pay your fare and go.

DIONYSUS
                              Here you are, one dollar.   270

(DIONYSUS *disembarks, and* CHARON *rows off. The scene is now the shore of the Underworld.*)

DIONYSUS (*peering nervously through the darkness*)
Xanthias! Where are you, Xanthias? Is that you, Xanthias?

XANTHIAS (*off*)
Oooooh!

DIONYSUS
            Over here!

(XANTHIAS *staggers in.*)

XANTHIAS
                        Oh master, I'm glad to see you.

DIONYSUS
What have we here?

XANTHIAS
                        Darkness and mud.

DIONYSUS
Did you see any juvenile delinquents here,

Or breakers of promises, as he said we should?

XANTHIAS
Why, don't you?

DIONYSUS (*pointing at the audience*)
Yes, there they are!
Well, what are we going to do?

XANTHIAS
                              Move farther on.
This is the place that Heracles said
Was full of monsters.

DIONYSUS (*boastfully*)
He'll be sorry he said it!
He was exaggerating just to scare me.
He knew I was brave, and hated competition.   280
Oh, he's the chieftain o' the puddin' race!
All I want now is for something to happen,
An adventure to make our trip worth while!

XANTHIAS
I bet you would. (*pretending he sees something*)
                              I can hear something moving!

DIONYSUS
Eeek! Where is it?

XANTHIAS
                              Behind us!

DIONYSUS
                                        Then get behind!

XANTHIAS
Now it's in front of us!

DIONYSUS
                              Get in front then!

XANTHIAS
Wow! I can see it! It's a great big monster!

DIONYSUS
What's it like?

XANTHIAS
                    Terrible; it keeps on changing!
Now it's a bull; now it's a mule;
And now it's a beautiful woman!

DIONYSUS (*leaping up*)
                              She's mine!   290

XANTHIAS
Stop! It's not a girl any longer, it's a dog!

DIONYSUS
It must be the Bogeyman!

XANTHIAS
                              Yes, there are flames
All round its head.

DIONYSUS
                    Has it one brass leg?

XANTHIAS
Yes, and another of cowdung! You're right!

DIONYSUS
Oh, where can I hide?

XANTHIAS
                    And where can I?

DIONYSUS
Now is the time for all good men to come to the aid of the party!

XANTHIAS
Great Heracles, this is it!

DIONYSUS
                    For heaven's sake
Keep your mouth shut, don't mention that name here!

XANTHIAS
Dionysus then!

DIONYSUS

That's even worse!

XANTHIAS (*pretending to exorcise the monster*)
Get thee behind me! Master, here, come here!

DIONYSUS
What's happening?

XANTHIAS

Everything's all right.   300
Now we can say, as the nervous speaker said,
It's a long lane that has no silver lining.
The Bogeyman's gone.

DIONYSUS

Swear it.

XANTHIAS

I swear.

DIONYSUS
Swear it again.

XANTHIAS
I swear.

DIONYSUS

And again.

XANTHIAS

I swear.

DIONYSUS
Oh dear! The sight of her made me go quite white!

XANTHIAS (*inspecting him*)
That all depends which way you look at it.

DIONYSUS (*in tragic mood*)
Oh gods, oh gods, look not so fierce upon me!
What is the cause, what is the cause, my soul?

XANTHIAS (*sarcastically*)
God's cabin in the skies, or marching Time?

(*A flute is heard offstage.*)

Master!

>DIONYSUS
>> What is it?

>XANTHIAS
>>> Didn't you hear it?

>DIONYSUS
>>>> What?   310

>XANTHIAS
>The breath of flutes.

>DIONYSUS
>>> Why yes; and I caught a whiff
>Of torches, all most mystical!
>Let's crouch down quietly, and hear the music.

>CHORUS (*off*)
>Iacchus, O Iacchus,
>Iacchus, O Iacchus!

>XANTHIAS
>That's it, master! Those are the Initiated
>He told us of, celebrating nearby.
>At least, that's the old Iacchus song they're singing.

>DIONYSUS
>I believe you're right. The best thing we can do
>Is wait and listen, till we know for certain.   320

(*Enter the* CHORUS OF INITIATED. *They wear holiday clothes, wreathes and garlands, and carry lighted torches.*)

>CHORUS
>Lord Iacchus, god most high,
>We who live here in your shadow
>Call on you, Iacchus, come,
>Nimble-footed through the meadow!
>Shake the crown of myrtle-berries

    Richly clustered round your head,
    Come, my lord, be mad and merry,
    In rites uninhibited.
    Come, Iacchus, show your paces
    In the holy mystic dance;   330
    Here's not one but many Graces
    Where the holy choirs advance.

XANTHIAS

Oh, by the holy daughter of Demeter,
What a wonderful smell of roast pork.

DIONYSUS

Shut up, and perhaps you'll get a sausage.

CHORUS

    Lord Iacchus, you are come,
    Daystar of our nightly band!
    Fires are blazing through the meadow,
    Lift your torches high in hand.
    In your holy ministration   340
    Old men lose the weight of years,
    Leaping high in exultation,
    Shedding all their cares and fears.
    Come, Iacchus, guide our way,
    Lead us to the flowery plain;
    Gone the cares of everyday,
    All are now made young again!

(*The procession comes to a halt, and the* CHORUS LEADER *delivers the ritual proclamation.*)

LEADER

Now is the time for a holy hush; let everyone leave our rites
Who has hardened his heart to our sacred words, never worshipped the Muse o' nights;
Who has never communed in spirit or flesh with great poets of bygone days,   350

Or the man whose delight is to make silly jokes, regardless of time
    or place;
Or the man who fans smouldering party strife with an eye to his
    personal profit
And cares not a bit for the good of the state, provided he makes
    something of it;
Or the leader of state who is open to bribes at a moment of na-
    tional crisis
And surrenders a ship or a garrison town for the sake of the mone-
    tary prizes;
Or the customs official who's deaf to the call of his five-per-cent
    duty, and sends
Prohibited goods through a neutral port, to further our enemies'
    ends;
Or the traitor who tries to procure supplies for the use of the en-
    emy fleet,
Or the man who takes part in a civic parade and relieves himself
    in the street;
Or the socialist leader who loudly insists that all men should have
    better pay   360
And reduces the dramatists' royalties when he has just been bur-
    lesqued in a play.
Depart from our rites! Depart, I say! I give you a final warning!
And the rest of you join in our festival songs, for we're not going
    home until morning!

CHORUS
Lift up your hearts, and go your way
To fair fields carpeted with flowers,
And while away the hours
In merry dance and play,
And laugh and jest the time away,
For we have eaten well today.

Go forward, let your song be heard   370
And praise the Goddess of Salvation,
Preserver of our nation

According to her word;
For she will never be deterred
By any of the common herd.

LEADER

Another hymn now; let's change our tune, and sing to Demeter
  instead,
And honor the goddess of growing things, who gives us our daily
  bread!

CHORUS

Come, Demeter, be our guide,
Over our glad rites preside;
Keep all evil things away,   380
Grant that I may all the day
Laugh and sing and mock and play.

Give me many things to say,
Something grave and something gay,
Worthy of your sacred feast;
Let us laugh and mock and jest
Till the critics give us best.

LEADER

Now call upon the boy-god, and honor him with song
Who travels with his revellers the sacred way along!

CHORUS

Iacchus, creator of festival song,   390
Come to the goddess and stand at her side,
Unwearied although you have travelled for long;
Iacchus, reveller, be our guide!

We've second-hand costumes and holes in our shoes;
It's good for a laugh and saves money besides!
But you give us *carte blanche* to insult whom we choose
Iacchus, reveller, be our guide!

Just now as the dancers went whirling about
A lovely young girl in their midst I espied
With a rip in her dress and her breast peeping out—   400

Iacchus, reveller, be our guide!

XANTHIAS
You know, whenever I see something like this
I always want to join in!

DIONYSUS
                    That goes for me too!
(*They move forward and join in the dance.*)

CHORUS
Archedemus is open to censures,
His passport's as false as his dentures.
He's the world's biggest fraud,
But the zombies applaud
And endorse his political ventures.

As for Cleisthenes, he's quite another matter.
In the graveyard you can hear his dismal chatter,   410
Where lamenting loud you'll find him
For the boy he left behind him
Without getting to the bottom of the latter.

Callias has joined the navy
Wrapped up in a lion's hide
But he's very much the lady
If you take a look inside.

DIONYSUS
Excuse me! Could you tell us where Pluto lives?
We're strangers here, and only just arrived.

CHORUS
It isn't far; you needn't ask again.   420
You're standing at his door and didn't know it.

DIONYSUS
Come on, pick up the bags again.

XANTHIAS
Here we go again! Tell me the old old story!

LEADER

Circle in your holy dances through the meadows thick with
  flowers
All of you who have a part in this our sacred festival.
I'll go with the women and the maidens, while
They keep their vigil, and display the sacred light!

CHORUS

On to banks where roses grow,
Where the flowers are thick and gay
Dancing our familiar way;   430
Happy Fates who willed it so.

Only we may see the sun,
Ours alone the holy light,
We who dwelt in ways of right
Evil offering to none!

(*The* CHORUS *move away, leaving* DIONYSUS *and* XANTHIAS *standing at the gate to the Underworld.* DIONYSUS' *courage has by this
time evaporated.*)

DIONYSUS

Now how should I knock on the door, I wonder?
What sort of knock is the custom hereabout?

XANTHIAS

Stop fooling around! Get your teeth into it!
Steal Heracles' thunder as well as his plunder!

DIONYSUS (*knocking timidly*)
Anyone at home?

AEACUS (*within*)
Who is it?

DIONYSUS
          Heracles the brave!   440

(*Enter* AEACUS.)

AEACUS

Well, Heracles, you low-down two-faced crook,

You stinking rotten pestilential skunk,
You're the one who ran off with our watchdog Cerberus,
Grabbed him by the throat, picked him up and bolted
When I was his keeper! Now I've got you where I want you.
Behold, the secret, black and midnight rock of Styx
And the blood-boltered pinnacles of Acheron
Confine you, and Cocytus' prowling hounds;
And the hundred-headed viper, which shall rend
Your entrails; on your lungs the venom'd eel   450
Of Tartessus shall batten, and your kidneys too
Teithrasian Gorgons soon shall tear asunder
And turn your guts into a bloody pulp.
On wingéd feet I fly to summon them!

(*Exit* AEACUS. *The sudden shock has proved too much for* DIONY-
sus' *self-control.*)

XANTHIAS
What's the matter?

DIONYSUS
                                    I've had an accident.

XANTHIAS
                                                      Gesundheit!
Get on your feet, you clown, and hurry,
Before somebody comes and sees you.

DIONYSUS
                                          Where am I?
Come on, put a cold wet sponge against my heart.

XANTHIAS
Here, catch, you do it. Ye golden gods!
Is that where your heart is?

DIONYSUS
                                    I was so scared   460
My heart was in my bowels.

XANTHIAS
Well, of all cowards human or divine
You take the prize.

DIONYSUS

Who, me?
A coward, just because I asked you for a sponge?
Now what would anybody else have done?

XANTHIAS

What?

DIONYSUS

A coward would have sat there wallowing in it.
I stood up straight away and wiped myself.

XANTHIAS

That took some courage.

DIONYSUS

I should say it did.
Weren't you afraid when you heard him sounding off
And bawling us out?

XANTHIAS

I didn't give it a thought!   470

DIONYSUS

Well, if you have an urge to show your courage
Catch hold of this club and lionskin of mine
And take my place, if you've got so much guts;
And I'll change parts with you and be the porter.

XANTHIAS

I haven't got much choice. Well; hand them over.
Now keep your eyes on Xanthiheracles
And see if he's as resourceful as you!

DIONYSUS

Oh, quite the tough guy, aren't we! Off you go.
I'll follow with the luggage.

(XANTHIAS *puts on the lionskin and takes the club, while* DIONYSUS *takes up the porter's pole. The gate opens again, and a* SERVANT *appears.*)

SERVANT

Oh Heracles honey, you're here! Come inside!   480

As soon as Madam heard you were coming
She set to work baking, boiled two or three
Tureens of soup, and barbecued an ox,
Made waffles and cookies—come along in!

XANTHIAS
Very kind, but no thank you.

SERVANT
                    But I can't let you
Go away, I really can't! She's making
A pot-roast of chicken and petits-fours
And decanting the finest wine in the house.
Come in!

XANTHIAS
            No thank you.

SERVANT
                You can't be serious.
I won't let you off. There's a flute-player
Waiting, and something else too—
Two or three dancing girls!

XANTHIAS
                Did you say dancing girls?

SERVANT
Just the right age, all fresh trimmed.

XANTHIAS
Well, just you go straight in and tell those dancing girls
That I intend to honor them with my presence.
Here, boy, pick up the luggage, follow me!

(XANTHIAS *is just about to follow the* SERVANT *off when* DIONYSUS
stops him.)

DIONYSUS
Here, not so fast! You can't be serious
Because I dressed you up as Heracles for fun?

Don't stand there talking nonsense, Xanthias.
Back to the luggage! Come on, pick it up!   500

XANTHIAS
What's this? You never mean to take away
What you just gave me?

DIONYSUS
                    Don't I just! I'm taking them!
Off with that lionskin!

XANTHIAS (*to the audience, as he is forcibly undressed*)
                              I hope you're all watching!
I leave it to the gods!

DIONYSUS
                    The gods indeed!
Why, how could you—what nonsense! what conceit!—
A slave, a mortal, pass for Heracles!

XANTHIAS
That's fine, you take them. I don't care. You might
Have need of me before long, heaven willing.

CHORUS
How sensible! How smart!   510
How like a man who knows his way around,
Not to make himself a fixture
Like a painted picture
But continually shift to better ground.
Cross over to the sunny side,
That's the clever thing to do;
It's the way that politicians make their money
And it seems to work for you.

DIONYSUS
Well, wouldn't it be ridiculous
To see them lay red carpets down for him,   520
Watch him flaunt himself before us
With a cutie from the chorus,

While I stood by to wait upon his whim?
When he saw me panting with emotion—
He's rogue enough for that, no doubt—
He might easily conceive a notion
To knock my ivory chatterers out!

(*Enter two* TAVERNKEEPERS *and their servants.*)

FIRST TAVERNKEEPER (*seeing* DIONYSUS *in the lionskin*)
Plathane, Plathane, here! There's the villain
Who came to our tavern before, and ate
Sixteen loaves of bread—

SECOND TAVERNKEEPER
     As I live and breathe,   53
That's the fellow.

XANTHIAS
    Here's trouble coming for somebody.

FIRST TAVERNKEEPER
And twenty plates of stew on top of that,
Firty cents apiece!

XANTHIAS
     Someone's in for it now!

FIRST TAVERNKEEPER
And mountains of pickles!

DIONYSUS
     What nonsense, woman!
You don't know what you're saying!

FIRST TAVERNKEEPER
       Did you think
I wouldn't recognize you in those fancy boots?
And I haven't said a word about that fish!

SECOND TAVERNKEEPER
And the dairy-fresh cheese the man gobbled up
Without even bothering to unwrap them first!

FIRST TAVERNKEEPER

And as soon as I so much as mentioned paying   540
He looked at me so fierce, and gave a bellow—

XANTHIAS

Yes, that's the way he always carries on!

FIRST TAVERNKEEPER

And drew his sword; I thought he was going mad!

SECOND TAVERNKEEPER

Oh, you poor dear!

FIRST TAVERNKEEPER

       And we were terrified
And ran away and hid behind the counter,
And he ran off and took the carpet with him!

XANTHIAS

Yes, that's just like him!

FIRST TAVERNKEEPER

       Something must be done.
You run along and find my attorney.

SECOND TAVERNKEEPER

And try to get hold of the union secretary!
We'll make him pay for this!

FIRST TAVERNKEEPER

       Old filthy guts!   550
I'd love to get a stone and smash your teeth in
For eating me out of house and home like that.

SECOND TAVERNKEEPER

I'd like a chance to bury him alive!

FIRST TAVERNKEEPER

I'd love to get a knife and cut his throat
For swallowing my tripe. I'll go and get
My attorney; he can slap a charge on him.
He'll wring it out of you today, he will!

(*Exeunt.*)

DIONYSUS (*his eye lighting on* XANTHIAS)
Perdition catch my soul, but I do love thee!

XANTHIAS
I know! I know what you're after! I don't want to hear
Another word. I won't be Heracles again!   56c

DIONYSUS
Oh Xanthy-Wanthy, don't be that way!

XANTHIAS (*sarcastically*)
                                        And how could I,
A slave, a mortal, pass for Heracles?

DIONYSUS
I know! I know you're angry, I don't blame you.
You could hit me and I wouldn't say a word.
But if ever I take them away from you again
A blight upon myself, my wife, my little ones,
My congressman.

XANTHIAS
I'll take your word. On those terms I'll be Heracles.

(*They exchange costumes again.*)

CHORUS
Now it's your responsibility
Since the uniform is yours once more   57c
To appear intimidating
Like the god you're imitating,
As pugnacious as you were before.
But if anybody catches you trembling
Or uttering a comic crack
That's the end of your dissembling;
To the bags you go straight back!

XANTHIAS
I'm very much obliged to you,
But the same idea occurred to me;
If he sees advantage in it   58c

He'll unfrock me in a minute,
That's a thing that any fool can see.
But I might as well play the hero
And put on my most peppery stare;
And I'd better be quick about it—
I can see somebody standing there!

(*Enter* AEACUS.)

AEACUS
Here, quickly, tie up this dog-thief!
Take him to jail!

DIONYSUS
Here's trouble on the way!

XANTHIAS
Don't you lay your hands on me!

AEACUS
You want to fight?
Here, Ditylas, Skebylas, Pardokas,   590
Come and give him what he's asking for!

(*Three thugs rush in and manhandle* XANTHIAS. DIONYSUS *watches
with interest.*)

DIONYSUS
How disgraceful! Resisting arrest!
And a thief into the bargain!

AEACUS
Monstrous!

DIONYSUS
Shocking! Disgraceful!

XANTHIAS
Now you listen here.
May I drop down dead if I've been here before
Or stolen anything from you worth a hair.
Come on, and I'll make a gentlemanly offer.
Take my slave, and give him the third degree.

If you prove me guilty you can take my life!

AEACUS
How shall I examine him?

XANTHIAS
                              Any way you like.   600
Strap him up, grill him, hang him, let him feel
The cat o' nine tails, take his hide off, rack him,
Pour vinegar up his nose, pile bricks on him,
Give him the works! I make one reservation:
Don't lash him with wet noodles.

AEACUS
                              Fair enough.
If we damage him in any way
Under examination, you'll be compensated.

XANTHIAS
Please don't mention it. Take him out and flog him.

AEACUS
I'll do it here, so you can watch him squeal.
Here you, put down that luggage, and take care   610
To tell nothing but the truth.

      DIONYSUS (*who has been growing steadily more agitated*)
                              Now listen here!
You can't flog me! I'm a god!
Go ahead at your peril!

AEACUS
                    What?

DIONYSUS
I tell you I'm a god—Dionysus, son of Zeus,
And this is my slave!

      AEACUS (*to* XANTHIAS)
                    You hear that?

XANTHIAS
                              I do.

All the more reason why he should be beaten.
If he's really a god he won't feel anything!

DIONYSUS
Yes, but you claim to be a god yourself!
You ought to get blow for blow with me!

XANTHIAS
Fair enough! (*to* AEACUS) Whichever one you see   620
First wincing or crying out, you can say
He's not the god!

AEACUS
Now there's a gentleman if I ever saw one!
You come to justice of your own accord.
Right, take off your clothes, both of you.

XANTHIAS
How can you test us fairly?

AEACUS
                         That's no problem.
I'll give you blow for blow.

XANTHIAS
                         That's fair enough.

(DIONYSUS *and* XANTHIAS *strip to the waist.* AEACUS *selects a large whip, then walks over and strikes* XANTHIAS, *who pretends not to notice.*)

AEACUS
There!

XANTHIAS
     Now watch me, see if I flinch!

AEACUS
But I've already hit you!

XANTHIAS
                    Have you? Really?   630

AEACUS
I'll have a go at the other one.

(*He crosses and strikes* DIONYSUS, *who similarly contains himself with an effort.*)

DIONYSUS
                              When?

AEACUS
I've done it!

DIONYSUS
                    I should have sneezed at least!

AEACUS (*puzzled*)
I'll try the other one again.

(*He crosses and strikes* XANTHIAS.)

XANTHIAS
                         Aaaaaaaah!

AEACUS
What's that? That one hurt!

XANTHIAS (*hastily improvising*)
I'm damned if it did!
I was thinking I had a feast day coming.

AEACUS
The man's a saint! Let's go over again. (*striking* DIONYSUS)

DIONYSUS
Yaaaaagh!

AEACUS
              What is it?

DIONYSUS (*pretending he sees something*)
                    Look! Men on horseback!

AEACUS (*suspiciously*)
What are you crying for?

DIONYSUS
                    Onions up my nose.

AEACUS
You didn't feel anything?

DIONYSUS
                    Me? You jest.   640

AEACUS
Well, I must go back to the other one. (*crossing to* XANTHIAS *and
striking him*)

XANTHIAS
Yaroo!

AEACUS
    What's that?

XANTHIAS
            There's a thorn in my foot!

AEACUS (*desperate*)
I CAN'T UNDERSTAND IT! Back we go.

(*He strikes* DIONYSUS, *who cannot control an oath; with great
presence of mind he turns it into a quotation.*)

DIONYSUS
Oh God . . . our help in ages past!

XANTHIAS
It hurt! Did you hear him?

DIONYSUS
                    It did no such thing.
I was merely quoting the first line of a hymn.

XANTHIAS
You're not getting anywhere. Cut him on the flank.

AEACUS
A good idea. (*crossing to* XANTHIAS)
Here, stick your stomach out! (*striking him*)

XANTHIAS
Heaven! Help!

DIONYSUS

  Somebody's crying!

XANTHIAS (*using* DIONYSUS' *technique*)
Heaven help the sailors on a night like this!   650

  AEACUS

Now by the powers above, I haven't a clue
Which one of you is the god. Both come inside;
My master will recognize you easily
And his queen Persephone; they're gods themselves.

  DIONYSUS

An excellent idea. I could have wished
You'd thought of it before I took that beating.

(*Exeunt.*)

  CHORUS

  Muse, make part of our sacred chorus,
  Come down and dance to the sound of our song.
  Look on the multitude here assembled
  To whom all wisdom and wit belong,   660
  Of nobler sort than Cleophon,
  That mongrel magpie, can ever own,
  Who snug in his alien hedgerow sits
  And whines away through his gibbering lips
  That no matter how equal the votes turn out
  He'll get the unbenefit of the doubt.

(*The* CHORUS *moves forward and addresses itself directly to the audience.*)

  The chorus has a god-appointed function
  To give the state political instruction.
  This is the first point of our declaration:
  NO REPRISALS and NO DISCRIMINATION.   670
  If anyone's been gulled by propaganda
  Let him state his case. No punishment, no slander.
  Second, RESTORE THE FRANCHISE. It's preposterous

That men who only fought one action should be naturalized,
    while better men are losterus.
Don't get me wrong! These New Citizens, I'm for 'em;
But others have fought for you for years, and their fathers
    before 'em.
So they made one slip. So what? So now they're penitent.
Be your age; stop sulking; show some family senniment.
We need anybody who can tell one end of an oar from the
    other,
So let's make every man of them a paid-up citizen and
    brother.   680
If you stand on your dignity while your city's being flattened
It won't be long before you wish you haddened.

If I'm any judge of a man's career
And can tell who'll suffer, and in what way,
That niggledy-piggledy lavatory man
Who lords it over his soap all day—
Yes, Cleigenes, that chimpanzee,
Won't bother us much any more, you'll see!
And because he knows where the danger lies
He tries to pull war-clouds over our eyes;   690
For once he has lost diplomatic immunity
He'll be set on when drunk, and stripped bare with im-
    punity.

It's the same with solid citizens as with our currency;
Both are calculated to induce despunnency.
It's not that we don't have enough good coinage
Free from counterfeitry and purloinage,
Mint-guaranteed, without a trace of fraud,
Honored at home, hard currency abroad.
But we never use it! We would rather settle
For second-rate adulterated metal,   700
Struck yesterday! We have men of reputation,
Sober and honest, with a liberal education,
But we maltreat them! and our state relies

On wetbacks, not greenbacks, alloys, not allies.
You idiots, return to proper courses,
Honor the men who are your best resources.
If you succeed, the world will sing your praise;
If not, you chose a noble way to end your days.

(*Enter* AEACUS *and* XANTHIAS. *The former is now much more affable.*)

AEACUS
So help me, he's a proper gentleman,
That master of yours.

XANTHIAS
                      A gentleman! I should think so!   710
There's nothing in his head but wine and women.

AEACUS
But not to beat you when they found you out,
A slave masquerading as his master!

XANTHIAS
He'd have been sorry!

AEACUS
                      That's the right way
For a slave to talk. I love it myself.

XANTHIAS
Love what?

AEACUS
          I'm in my seventh heaven
When I can swear at my master behind his back.

XANTHIAS
And what about muttering under your breath
When you leave the room after a beating?

AEACUS
                                    That's swell!

XANTHIAS
And poking your nose in his business?   720

AEACUS
That beats everything!

XANTHIAS
                        Brother of mine! And what about
Overhearing master's secrets?

AEACUS
                        It sends me wild!

XANTHIAS
And repeating them to the neighbors?

AEACUS
Why, when I do that, I'm hysterical!

XANTHIAS
Let me shake your hand! Come, kiss and make friends.

(A *confused noise of shouting is heard off stage.*)

But tell me, by the patron saint of thieves,
What's all that noise and shouting inside,
And all those catcalls?

AEACUS
                        Aeschylus and Euripides.

XANTHIAS
Eh?

AEACUS
        Yes, this is an event, a great event
In the Underworld, all the dead are taking sides.   730

XANTHIAS
What about?

AEACUS
                We have a law among us here
About the arts, the foremost liberal arts—
That the foremost master in each art
Shall have free dinners in the city hall
And have a chair of honor next to Pluto—

XANTHIAS

                                        Oh, I see.

AEACUS

—until somebody else should come along
More talented, and then he must back down.

XANTHIAS

But why should this have bothered Aeschylus?

AEACUS

Aeschylus held the throne of tragedy
As being the greatest master of that art.   740

XANTHIAS

And now?

AEACUS

            Why, when Euripides came down
He showed off to the hijackers and pickpockets,
The burglars and the juvenile delinquents,
The rabble of Hades. And when they heard
His repartee and twists and paradoxes
They all went crazy, hailed him as the Master;
It went to his head, and he laid hands on the throne
Where Aeschylus sat.

XANTHIAS

                        And wasn't pelted off?

AEACUS

Not a bit! The public demanded a trial
To see which one had the greater talent.   750

XANTHIAS

All the rabble, you mean?

AEACUS

                        That's right! They raised the roof!

XANTHIAS

But didn't Aeschylus have any supporters?

AEACUS

Honest men are hard to come by (*pointing to the audience*) just
like here!

XANTHIAS

Well, what does Pluto mean to do about it?

AEACUS

To hold a competition, a trial of skill
In writing tragedies!

XANTHIAS

But what about Sophocles?
Why didn't he make a bid for the throne?

AEACUS

Oh no, not him! As soon as he arrived
He saluted Aeschylus and shook his hand
And waived his claim to the throne, that's what he did.   760
But we hear from his leading man that he's going
To sit in Aeschylus' corner; if he wins
Then Sophocles will retire, but if he doesn't
He says he'll fight Euripides for the title.

XANTHIAS

Will it come off?

AEACUS

Yes, any minute now.
And then there'll be some wonderful goings on.
They'll weigh poetic genius in scales—

XANTHIAS

What, weigh out tragedy like butcher's meat?

AEACUS

They'll bring their footrules and their measuring tapes
And wooden squares—

XANTHIAS

Why, are they making bricks?   770

AEACUS

—and wedges and compasses; Euripides
Swears that he'll test the tragedies word by word.

XANTHIAS

I bet Aeschylus took it badly.

AEACUS

He looked wild!
He tossed his head like a bull!

XANTHIAS

And who's to be judge?

AEACUS

That was the difficulty.
They couldn't find any knowledgeable critics.
Aeschylus hated the Athenians—

XANTHIAS

Thought there were too many jailbirds there, perhaps!

AEACUS

—and said that no-one else was worth a cent
When it came to judging poetic genius.   780
But in the end they left it to your master.
After all, he's an expert. Come on, let's go in.
When the masters have got business on their minds
The slaves must take the kicks!

(*Exeunt.*)

CHORUS

Imagine the roarer's implacable wrath
And his furious rolling of eyes at the sight
Of his rattle-tongued rival upreared in his path
And whetting his tusks for the fight!

Now helmets will shatter and feathers will fly
And chariots splinter their wheels in the press   790
When the high-stepping words of the moulder of minds
Are matched against subtle finesse!

His great shaggy mane will rise upon his neck,
He'll wrinkle his brows in a thundersome frown
And send masses of words in a hurricane blast
Like ship's timbers tumbling down!

In answer the garrulous wielder of words
Will unwind his sophistical critical tongue,
Give rein to his malice and probe and dissect
This prodigious labor of lung!   800

(*The scene changes to a hall in* PLUTO's *palace. Enter* DIONYSUS
and PLUTO *as judges, and* AESCHYLUS *and* EURIPIDES *in fierce argument.*)

EURIPIDES
I won't give up the throne, don't talk to me!
I tell you I'm a better poet than he is!

(AESCHYLUS *turns away in disdain.*)

DIONYSUS
You hear him, Aeschylus, why don't you answer?

EURIPIDES
He's beginning with his high-and-mighty act,
The way he used to bluff us in his tragedies!

DIONYSUS
Now listen genius, don't talk too big!

EURIPIDES
Oh, I know him! I saw through him ages ago!
Bard of the wide open spaces, leather-lunged,
His mouth undoored, unbridled, uncontrolled,
Uncircumlocutionary, rodomontadian!   810

AESCHYLUS
Is that so? You child of the cabbage patch!
To talk to me like that, you gossipophilist,
You pauper-poet, patchwork-versifier!
You won't get away with this!

DIONYSUS

                           Stop, Aeschylus!
Don't work yourself into a flaming temper!

AESCHYLUS

Not till I've shown him up for what he is,
This cripple-maker, for all his boasting!

DIONYSUS

Here, boys, we'd better take some storm precautions.
It looks as though a hurricane's blowing up.

AESCHYLUS (*to* EURIPIDES)

You and your lewd mimes and cancan dances,   820
And plays about adultery and incest!

DIONYSUS

Here, hold your horses, venerable Aeschylus!
And you, Euripides, if you've any sense,
Get under cover till the hailstorm's over,
Or else some heady word flung out in anger
Will crack your skull and spill your "Beggar Prince."
Now don't be in a fury, Aeschylus, but submit
To question and answer calmly. It's undignified
For poets to howl abuse at each other like two fishwives!
But there you go, roaring like a forest fire!   830

EURIPIDES

Well, I'm quite ready, without reservations,
To bite first or be bitten, as he likes.
Here are my dialogues, my lyrics and my plots,
My "Murderer at Large," my "Incestuous Marriage,"
My "Death by Proxy" and my "Beggar Prince," of course.

DIONYSUS

Well, Aeschylus, tell us, what do you want to do?

AESCHYLUS

I could have wished the trial had been somewhere else.
He has the advantage of me here.

DIONYSUS

How's that?

AESCHYLUS

MY poetry didn't die with me.
His did. He has it all here to recite.   840
But all the same, I'm ready, if you wish.

DIONYSUS

Let someone bring me frankincense and fire,
And let me pray before they show their wit
To judge them by the highest laws of poetry.
And while I pray, an anthem to the Muses!

CHORUS

Celestial Muses, nine daughters of god,
Who preside over weavers of phrases,
Men of trenchant perception and razor-edged wit,
Come and see them both put through their paces!
As they meet in the thrust and riposte of debate,   850
Each gingerly testing the other man's weight,
And display their poetical graces
With lines that are bold and emphatic
Or brilliantly epigrammatic;
In a minute or two
We'll begin to see who
Is the master in matters dramatic!

DIONYSUS (*to the poets*)
Now you two pray, before you show your lines.

AESCHYLUS (*in high liturgical tone*)
Demeter, thou who nourishest my thought,
Come, make me worthy of thy mysteries!   860

DIONYSUS (*to* EURIPIDES)
You throw on a pinch of incense too!

EURIPIDES (*contemptuously*)
No thanks! I pray to quite a different sort of god.

DIONYSUS

Your own coinage, eh?

EURIPIDES

That's right! I invented them myself!

DIONYSUS

Well, pray away then to your—irregulars!

EURIPIDES

O air, my sustenance, and clacking tongue
And intellect and penetrating nose
Grant that I floor his every argument!

CHORUS

We're bursting with anticipation
To hear what the clever men say,
With what manner of argumentation   870
They walk their irascible way!
There's little of reticence in them,
Stupidity notably less;
I wonder how each will begin, then?
Perhaps I can hazard a guess!
The one will be pithy and pointed,
The other descend with a roar
On his epigrams, leave them disjointed
And scattered all over the floor!

DIONYSUS

Now speak with all the wit you may. I warn you, I've an allergy   880
To platitude and cliché and elaborate analogy!

EURIPIDES

I'll defer examination of my own poetic genius; for the moment
      let me concentrate on his—
Show you how he fooled a public that was raised on blood-and-
      thunder, and expose him for the phoney that he is!
He would open his performance with a solitary character, a hero-
      ine or hero in a veil
Who would sit like so much scenery and never say a syllable—

DIONYSUS

That's right!

EURIPIDES

                    —and then the chorus starts to wail
Four interminable stanzas in consecutive succession, and the ac-
    tor sat and never said a word.

DIONYSUS

But I somehow loved that silence, it was far more satisfactory
    than all this modern chatter!

EURIPIDES

                    That's absurd!

DIONYSUS

I defer to your opinion; but whatever made him do it?

EURIPIDES

It was bluff, to keep the audience in suspense,
Wondering when her mouth would open; and meanwhile the
    plot's unrolling.

DIONYSUS

                    Well, I was fooled! (*to* AESCHYLUS, *who shows
signs of impatience*) No need to take offence!

EURIPIDES

I've hit him on a tender spot! Then after this baloney, when the
    play's already more than halfway through,   890
He'd pronounce a dozen wild and elephantine polysyllables, great
    Bugaboos with manes and eyebrows too,
Not in any dictionary.

AESCHYLUS

                    What the—

DIONYSUS

                    Stop, don't grind your teeth!

EURIPIDES

You couldn't understand a single word he said—

Scamanders, moated camps, emblazoned targe and brazen griffin-
eagles, elevated miles above your head,
Incomprehensible!

DIONYSUS

I've often lain awake at night and wondered
just what sort of bird a tawny cockhorse was.

AESCHYLUS

You unmitigated idiot, it came in a description of a figurehead
upon a ship, of course!

(*To* EURIPIDES.)

And now perhaps you'll tell us, you offence that stinks to heaven,
of what nature were the tragedies you wrote?

EURIPIDES

I didn't take my matter out of oriental tapestries; no cockhorse
there, no beast half stag, half goat.
I inherited the art from you all dropsical and bloated, and inflated
with hot air and adipose,
So I put her on a diet, and reduced her weight with exercise, and
limericks, and daily purging dose,
And injections of periphrasis distilled from periodicals, and solos,
and a touch of servants' hall.
I didn't rave haphazardly, or rush into the thick of things; my first
appearing character gave all
The needful explanation of the drama's antecedents.

900

AESCHYLUS

More respectable than yours, I fondly hope!

EURIPIDES

There was never any let-up from the drama's opening verses; all
my characters conversed without a stop,
The masters and the mistresses, the grannies and domestics—

AESCHYLUS

And isn't that a capital offence?

EURIPIDES

The people have a right of self-expression!

DIONYSUS

That's a dangerous road
to follow; cut it out, if you have sense!

EURIPIDES

I employed the stage to demonstrate the art of public speaking—

AESCHYLUS

You did indeed! And I should have preferred
Your lungs had burst before you did!

EURIPIDES

I gave them rules and stand-
ards, and instructed them to question every word,
To worship ingenuity, make theories, be critical, not take on trust
a single thing they heard.
I wrote of ordinary scenes, of everyday occurrences, so they could
see at once if I was lying,
Never blustered on and took away their powers of criticism, never
wrote of clanging steeds and horses dying.   910
Consider our disciples and you'll see who is the better; his are
jingoistic, passé ineffectuals,
The sabre-rattling death-and-glory boys; I have the demagogues,
the foxy diplomats, the intellectuals!

DIONYSUS

I know your sort of diplomat: sophisticated, cynical, who watches
for the falling of the dice
And at any sign of trouble, when he's heading for disaster, he'll
transfer his own allegiance in a trice.

EURIPIDES

That's the sort of thing I taught them.
In my plays they found chop-logic,
How to question and examine,
How to put their house in order,
How to ask "What's going on here?"

"How is this?" and "What's the reason?"   920

DIONYSUS

True! Now every man in Athens
When he gets home from the office
Falls to bawling out the servants:
"Well, how did this vase get broken?
Who's been chewing this sardine-head?
Where's our year-old dinner service?
Has that garlic gone already?
Only yesterday I bought some.
Who's been nibbling at the olives?"
But before they took his teaching   930
They all sat with mouths wide open
Like a lot of mama's darlings!

CHORUS

Illustrious Achilles, remember!
Dismount from your very high horse!
Give answer but don't let your temper
Carry you outside the course.
He's made some bizarre accusations
But shorten your sails to the breeze;
Remember your dignified station
And weather the tempest with ease!   940
Look out for the wind when it's dropping
And bring your ship under his bow;
If you'd catch Euripides hopping
You'll need clever seamanship now!

DIONYSUS

Now Aeschylus, our founder of high tragic declamation and
    adorner of theatrical pomposity,
First figure in our drama, speak with neither fear nor favor, and
    let loose the pent-up floods of your verbosity!

AESCHYLUS

My position is invidious; I think myself insulted to be questioned
    by a character like this,

But he mustn't be permitted to allege he left me speechless! So
   I'll ask you, sir, what quality it is
That makes a poet admirable?

EURIPIDES

                       Cleverness, and good advice, and

making better citizens.

AESCHYLUS

             Of course!
And suppose you've done the opposite, and taken honest gentle-
   men and turned them into criminals or worse?   950
What's the penalty for that?

DIONYSUS

              Why, death, don't ask him!

AESCHYLUS
Then consider how I left them under my administration—
Good six-footers every man of 'em, not layabouts and runaways
   and hoodlums like the present generation.
Their whole life was swords and battle-axes, nodding snow-white
   helmet feathers, casques and greaves and armor-plated passion—

EURIPIDES
There, you see, he's off already!

DIONYSUS

                I can't hear for all this metal-

beating!

EURIPIDES
      What did you do, pray, to start this fashion?

(AESCHYLUS *looks offended.*)

DIONYSUS
Come on, don't be so confoundedly standoffish!

AESCHYLUS

                   I composed an

epic drama full of war.

EURIPIDES

What was the story?

AESCHYLUS

"The Seven Against Thebes," and every man who came to see it
went home burning with desire for martial glory!

DIONYSUS

So it's you we have to thank for it! On that account at any rate
you ought to have a beating, yes, and more,
For because you wrote a play about them every single Theban's
grown courageous and more resolute for war.

AESCHYLUS

And you could have emulated them, but followed other courses.
Then I honored a magnificent achievement
With my "Persians," firing citizens with patriotic ardor—

DIONYSUS

I recall the chorus moaning in bereavement   960
As they stood around Darius' tomb, yelled "Yowoi" and gesticu-
lated. How it warmed the cockles of my heart!

AESCHYLUS

That's the proper stuff of poetry. Consider how our poets brought
us good advice and blessings from the start.
First came Orpheus to establish our religious celebrations and instruct us to restrain our hands from killing,
Then Musaeus taught us healing and prophetic divination, and
old Hesiod the arts of ploughing, tilling
And of garnering our harvest. Then came Homer, the immortal:
how did he acquire his honor and his name
Save by teaching high accomplishments, and battle drill, and
strategy, and bravery, and military fame?

DIONYSUS

Well, he hadn't taught the officer that I was watching yesterday,
on parade and just that minute out of bed
With his helmet-plume in hand, and he was trying to affix it when
his helmet was already on his head!

AESCHYLUS

But he wrote of other heroes of whom some are still among us,
   and from him my inspiration started flowing,
So I wrote of mighty warriors as models for the citizens whenever
   they should hear the trumpet blowing;   970
I didn't write of hussies or adulterous entanglements; I never
   showed a heroine in love!

EURIPIDES

No, you never had the smallest touch of Venus!

AESCHYLUS

                              May I never!

But you and yours and she were hand in glove
Till at last she threw you over!

DIONYSUS

                    That's a shrewd one!

AESCHYLUS

You wrote plays about adultery and husbands taken in,
Preaching while your wife was practising!

EURIPIDES (*controlling himself with an effort*)

                              How have I harmed the

citizens by writing of adultery and sin?

AESCHYLUS

There are scores of honest gentlewomen, wives of decent husbands, who've been driven into suicide by you,
For your scenes of lust and passion so ashamed them they took
   poison—

EURIPIDES

            And isn't every word I've written true?

AESCHYLUS

Oh, it's realistic, granted! But a poet shouldn't publish promis-
   cuity and moral degradation;
Little boys they go to school and pay attention to the teacher;
   but the poet is the teacher of the nation!

The poet should confine himself to moral and uplifting sub-
jects—

AESCHYLUS

EURIPIDES
        Does it seem uplifting, then, to you,
To make every word a mountain, to converse in blocks of granite,
    when you ought to speak as human beings do?   980

AESCHYLUS
You numskull, when the themes are elevated, and the concept,
    then the language should be elevated too!
And superhuman characters use superhuman language—after all,
    they dress more grandly than we do!
But you took my high conception and degraded it—

EURIPIDES

                                        How did I?

AESCHYLUS
By costuming tragic kings in rags and tatters
To create a moving spectacle—

EURIPIDES
                Why shouldn't I?

AESCHYLUS
                        Your rich men
    have employed the same technique in public matters.
For nobody is willing now to pay his corporate taxes; he'll put on
    a suit of rags and say he's famished.

DIONYSUS
But underneath his rags he wears a custom-tailored undershirt,
    eats caviar when the tax-collector's vanished!

AESCHYLUS
He instructed them to chatter and to love the sound of argument,
    and emptied all the playing-fields, and taught
The sailors to dispute their captain's orders; but in my time never
    any sailor had a single thought
But of calling for his rations and of singing yohoho!

DIONYSUS

And of spitting on the fellow in the porthole down below,   990
And of pillaging the natives every time they went ashore;
Now they yarn away in harbor, no-one's rowing any more!

AESCHYLUS

That's the sort of thing he taught them;
In his plays you'll find white slavers,
Sisters married to their brothers,
Women giving birth in temples,
Saying life is non-existence.
That's the reason why our city's
Full of petty bureaucratic
Socialistic fellow-travellers   1000
Making monkeys of the public!
No-one's fit to run the torch-race!

DIONYSUS

Yes, I split my sides with laughing
At the State Fair races, when I
Saw a runner bending double,
Fat and puffed and having trouble,
Last of all the field; and when the
Potters saw him from the archway
Out they came and slapped his bottom
And his flanks and chest and tummy;   1010
He so huffed and puffed and panted
With the beating he was getting
He puffed out his torch and vanished!

CHORUS

Here's a hard-fought battle, here's a most exciting fight,
It's impossible at present to say who is in the right;
When one comes storming in the other feints and never flinches,
And shows his nimble footwork; now breaks quickly from the
    clinches!
There are many other tricks and opportunities for wit
So fight in any way you know, and give and take and hit,

Many old and new devices, many subtle *jeux d'esprit*;   1020
And if you fear your audience's capability
To understand your meaning, you need have no fear for them—
After all, they're all intelligent and educated men!
They've been on many forays into literary matters
And brought their books along so they can understand the patter,
So take courage and go forward! Many subtleties await us!
Be as smart as you know how, for you have many smart spectators!

EURIPIDES

Very well! I'll turn my attention to his prologues,
And begin my inquisition of this genius
With the beginnings of his tragedies.   1030
He always was unclear in exposition.

DIONYSUS

Which one will you examine?

EURIPIDES

Lots of them!
First quote me that one from the "Oresteia," please.

DIONYSUS

Silence in court! Now Aeschylus, speak up.

AESCHYLUS

"Dark Hermes, guardian of father's rights,
I pray that thou may be my guide and savior,
For I return, and to my land am come...."

DIONYSUS

Do you find any faults in that?

EURIPIDES

A dozen or more!

DIONYSUS

But there were only three lines altogether!

EURIPIDES

But every one has twenty errors in it!   1040

(AESCHYLUS *begins to protest.*)

DIONYSUS
Aeschylus, I should advise you to be quiet,
Or else you'll end up owing more than three lines' worth!

AESCHYLUS
Be quiet? I? For him?

DIONYSUS
                              I strongly recommend it.

EURIPIDES
He's made a colossal blunder straight away.

AESCHYLUS
You don't know what you're talking about!

EURIPIDES
                                        Who cares?

AESCHYLUS
Well, what mistakes?

EURIPIDES
                        Please quote the lines again.

AESCHYLUS
"Dark Hermes, guardian of father's rights...."

EURIPIDES
I believe those lines are spoken by Orestes
Over his murdered father's tomb?

AESCHYLUS
                        Correct.

EURIPIDES
He calls on Hermes, when his father had been killed   1050
Brutally and cold-bloodedly by his wife
And calls him "Guardian of father's rights"?

AESCHYLUS
He doesn't mean that at all! He calls on Hermes
In his function of conductor of dead souls
And makes it clear that he inherited

That function from his father—*Hermes'* father—Zeus!

EURIPIDES
In that case he made a bigger blunder than I thought!
If Hermes inherited that function from his father—

DIONYSUS
He'd be a body-snatcher on his father's side!

AESCHYLUS
Dionysus, you can save your stinking breath!   1060

DIONYSUS
You go on quoting! (*to* EURIPIDES) And you watch out for errors!

AESCHYLUS
"I pray that thou may be my guide and savior,
For I return, and to my land am come."

EURIPIDES
Our clever Aeschylus repeats himself!

DIONYSUS
How?

EURIPIDES
      Look at what he says, and I'll explain.
"For I return" he says "and to my land am come."
"To come" and "to return" are synonyms!

DIONYSUS
Exactly! Just as if I were to ask my neighbor
"Lend me a frying pan, or else a griddle!"

AESCHYLUS
I tell you the words aren't the same at all!   1070
You numskull, my phraseology is perfect!

DIONYSUS
I'd be glad if you could tell me what you mean.

AESCHYLUS
Why, anyone who has a home can come to it.
He comes; it has no other implication.

An exile both comes home and returns to it!

DIONYSUS
Yes, very clever! What do you say to that?

EURIPIDES
I don't admit Orestes did return.
He came in secret, without the proper papers.

DIONYSUS
That's clever too. I can't understand a word.

EURIPIDES
Go on and quote some more.

DIONYSUS
                              Yes, go on, Aeschylus,   1080
And hurry up. And you watch out for faults.

AESCHYLUS
"Here on this high-built tomb I call my father
To hear, to listen—"

EURIPIDES
                         There he goes again!
"To hear, to listen"—obviously identical!

DIONYSUS
He was talking to the dead, you idiot!
You have to call on them at least three times!

AESCHYLUS
Well, how did you write prologues?

EURIPIDES
                                    You shall see!
And if you find there any repetition
Or any padding, you may spit on me!

DIONYSUS
Well, quote away; after all, that's what I'm here for,   1090
To judge the merits of your prologue writing.

EURIPIDES

"A happy man was Oedipus at first—"

AESCHYLUS

He was no such thing! As unhappy as he could be!
Before he was born, before he was even thought of,
It was prophesied that he should kill his father.
How could he be a happy man at first?

EURIPIDES

"And then became most wretched of mankind—"

AESCHYLUS

I deny it! He was never anything else!
As soon as he was born they threw him out
In a jug, and this was in the depths of winter,   1100
To stop him growing up to kill his father.
And then with ankles pierced he crawled to Polybus,
And in his teens he married an old woman
Who on top of that turned out to be his mother!
And then he blinded himself!

DIONYSUS

                                    All he needed
Was to be court-martialed for it afterwards!

EURIPIDES

You're talking nonsense! My prologues are all right!

AESCHYLUS

So help me, I won't go pecking word by word
At every single phrase! With heaven's aid
I'll take an oil-can and explode your prologues!   1110

EURIPIDES

My prologues? With an oil-can?

AESCHYLUS

                                    Just one oil-can!
You write them so that everything fits in—
Bedspread, handbag, oil-can—anything

Can be adapted to your tragic lines!
Quote, and I'll prove it!

EURIPIDES

You'll prove it! Really!

AESCHYLUS

Yes!

DIONYSUS
Euripides, we're waiting for you!

EURIPIDES
"Aegyptus, as the legends mostly tell,
With fifty sons the foaming ocean crossed
But reaching Argos—"

AESCHYLUS

Had his oil-can lost!

EURIPIDES
What's this about the oil-can, damn and blast it?   1120

DIONYSUS
Quote him another; I haven't got it yet.

EURIPIDES
"Dionysus, dancing on Parnassus' peak
With sacred wand, and wrapped in skin of deer
By torchlight—"

AESCHYLUS

Saw his oil-can disappear!

DIONYSUS
Help! Once again the oil-can's knocked us flat!

EURIPIDES
Don't let it worry you! Here's another one
Without a crack to stick the oil-can in!
"There is no man who's blessed in everything.
One, high-born, for a pittance needs must toil,
The other, low-born—"

AESCHYLUS

Lost his can of oil!   1130

DIONYSUS

Euripides!

EURIPIDES

What is it?

DIONYSUS

Take in canvas!
This oil-can's blowing up a hurricane!

EURIPIDES

I wouldn't even think of such a thing!
I'll knock it from his hands in half a minute!

DIONYSUS

Well, quote another—and watch out for oil-cans!

EURIPIDES

"Time was when Cadmus, great Agenor's son,
Sailing to Sidon—"

AESCHYLUS

Found his oil-can gone!

DIONYSUS

Euripides, dear boy! Why don't you buy the thing
Before it shatters all our prologues?

EURIPIDES

Buy it?
You can't be serious!

DIONYSUS

I'm telling you!   1140

EURIPIDES

Not yet! I still have plenty of prologues left
Where he won't be able to stick the oil-can in!
"Pelops to Pisa once his way did wind
On horseback—"

AESCHYLUS
>And left his can of oil behind!

DIONYSUS
Just look at that! Here comes the thing again!
Make him an offer for it while there's time!
You'll get it for a quarter, it's a bargain!

EURIPIDES
Not yet, by heaven; here are plenty more.
"King Oineus from the soil—"

AESCHYLUS
>Has lost his can of oil!

EURIPIDES
DON'T INTERRUPT ME HALFWAY THROUGH A LINE!   1150
"King Oineus from the soil good harvest won,
But giving thanks—"

AESCHYLUS
>He found his oil-can gone!

DIONYSUS
In the middle of a sacrifice? Who took it?

EURIPIDES
Be quiet! Let him try to cap this one!
"Zeus, as the tale is told by history—"

DIONYSUS
But where his oil-can's gone's a mystery!
That's how he'll cap it! You don't have a chance!
These oil-cans seem to grow upon your prologues
Like styes upon the eyes. For heaven's sake
Move over to his lyrics, and consider them!   1160

EURIPIDES
His lyrics! Yes, I'll show him up there, all right!
All his lyrics are exactly the same!

CHORUS
What in the world will he do?

I haven't the ghost of a notion
How he can condemn a man who
Has won universal devotion.
His lyrics are better than any,
He certainly wrote a good many!
There's nothing I fear you can criticize here,
Your chances are not worth a penny!   1170

EURIPIDES
Oh, wonderful songs! Let's have a look at them!
I'll show you how he used one meter for the lot!

DIONYSUS
I'll take a handful of pebbles and keep score.

(*Music.* EURIPIDES *sings.*)

EURIPIDES
"Achilles, can you hear the shock of heroes cut asunder?
Oho, there's a blow; captain, come to our assistance!
We who dwell beside the lake pray our forefather Hermes,
Oho, there's a blow; captain, come to our assistance!"

DIONYSUS
That's two blows for you, Aeschylus!

EURIPIDES
"Oh noblest of Achaeans, son of Atreus, hear my story!
Oho, there's a blow; captain, come to our assistance!"   1180

DIONYSUS
That's a third blow for you, Aeschylus!

EURIPIDES
"The keepers of the sacred bees are opening the temple,
Oho, there's a blow; captain, come to our assistance!
I have the power to tell about the fateful expedition,
Oho, there's a blow; captain, come to our assistance!"

DIONYSUS
Good gracious, what an awful lot of blows!
Excuse me, I must run along to the bathroom.
These blows have brought on my old kidney trouble!

EURIPIDES

Not till you've heard his other sort of songs,
The ones he wrote for lyre accompaniment!   1190

DIONYSUS

Well, sing some more; but let's have no more blows!

EURIPIDES (*singing*)

I'll tell how the furious eagle, with spear in avenging hand,
Tralalala tralala, tralalala trala,
Sends the twin rulers of Hellas, pride of the Grecian land,
Tralalala tralala, tralalala trala,
And the Sphinx, black bitch of ill-omen, maintaining her evil
    sway,
Tralalala tralala, tralalala trala,
Gave to the swift-flying hounds of heaven their lawful prey,
Tralalala tralala, tralalala trala,
And it all fell down upon Ajax,   1200
Tralalala trala!

DIONYSUS

What's all this tralala? A spinning song?
You certainly spun it out for long enough!

AESCHYLUS

I went to honest sources for my lyrics
And turned them all to honest purposes.
I didn't want to pick poetic blossoms
From gardens that my predecessors planted.
But he picks up his music anywhere—
From street-girls, drinking songs and funerals,
Dance halls and jazz bands. Listen, and you'll see.   1210
Bring me a lyre! No, wait; who wants a lyre
For tunes like these? Bring on the girl who plays
The castanets! Muse of Euripides,
Come forward! These songs require your talents!

(*Enter the* MUSE *of* EURIPIDES, *an old hag.*)

DIONYSUS

Well here's one Muse that can't be prostituted!

AESCHYLUS (*singing*)
Sweet is the squawk of the halcyon
Over the ceaseless sea,
Dabbling wings in the water,
Dew-dropping daintily.
Skillful the sport of the spiders   1220
Wiiiiiiiiiiiinding their webs in the roof:
Song of the shuttle,
How they scuttle!
Dulcet the dance of the dolphin
Merrily skipping
Before the shipping,
Is it the truth
That the stars foretell?
Will the horse I backed do well?
Let's drown our cares in wine   1230
And drink the grape divine;
Come kiss me quick, my love!
Do you see that foot?

DIONYSUS (*misunderstanding, and looking around on the
    floor*)
                    Oh yes!

AESCHYLUS
Aha! You see it, eh?

DIONYSUS
                    No doubt about it!

AESCHYLUS (*to* EURIPIDES)
This stuff has more false lines and platitudes
Than a prostitute has attitudes!
You dare to say my verse is flat
When you can write such trash as that?
Then so much for his lyrics; now I'll show you
How he composed his solos.   1240

(*Singing.*)

O sable night
What is this fright
You send me from the pit of Hell?
What is this dream?
I faint, I scream;
What is this vision fell?
Half dead and half alive,
Wrapped close in sombre veils,
With murder, murder in its eyes
And great big finger nails.   1250

Women, wake and light the lantern,
Warm me water from the stream;
Hurry, hurry, fill the basin,
Let me wash away my dream!

Well, what do you know?
Women, come and look!
My little maid servant has run off with my cock!
Nymphs of the rock, stop her do!

There I was sitting
Indoors with my knitting,   1260
My needles were busy and full,
And I thought of a day at the fair
And of selling my cockerel there,
And wound up a fresh ball of wool.

Into the air it flew, it flew,
Fluttered its feathers and fled,
Leaving me here so blue, so blue,
Nothing but tears, but tears to shed,
Nothing but tears to shed.

So bring your bows, you Cretans, come,   1270
Run to stand around her home;
Artemis, unleash your hounds,

Hunt with me through house and grounds;
Great moon goddess, light your lantern,
Lift your torches in the skies,
Send your rays into her dwelling
And let me catch her with her prize!

DIONYSUS
That's enough singing!

AESCHYLUS
                    I agree with you.
What I want is to bring him to the balance,
And this shall be our sole criterion—   1280
Which is the weightier, his verse or mine!

DIONYSUS
Well, come on then, if that's what I must do—
Weigh out poetic genius like cheese!

CHORUS
Genius is nine parts sweat,
Here's the greatest marvel yet!
Here's a prodigy of wit,
Who else would have thought of it?
Only seeing is believing;
If some passing stranger had
Told me, I'd have said "Deceiving   1290
Fellow, you must think I'm mad!"

(*As the* CHORUS *sings, a large pair of scales is lowered onto the stage.*)

DIONYSUS
Now take your places by the balance.

AESCHYLUS & EURIPIDES
                              Here we are!

DIONYSUS
Each of you speak a line into the scale,
And don't let go until I shout "Cuckoo!"

BOTH
We have it.

DIONYSUS
          Right, let's hear a line from each.

EURIPIDES
"If only the good ship Argo had never flown"

AESCHYLUS
"River Spercheius, where the cattle graze"

DIONYSUS
Cuckoo!

BOTH
          It's moving!

DIONYSUS
                    Aeschylus' scale goes down
Far lower.

EURIPIDES
          What can be the explanation?

DIONYSUS
He put in a river, the way wooldealers do,   1300
To water the goods and make them overweight!
Besides, you used a verse with wings on it!

EURIPIDES
Well, let him quote another, and we'll see!

DIONYSUS
Take hold again!

BOTH
          We've got it!

DIONYSUS
                    Quote!

EURIPIDES
"Persuasion has no temple but in speech."

AESCHYLUS
"Of all the gods, Death only asks no gifts."

DIONYSUS
Let go!

BOTH
    It's moving!

DIONYSUS
                His goes down again!
He threw in Death, the heaviest of burdens!

EURIPIDES
But my "Persuasion" was a perfect line!

DIONYSUS
Persuasion's hollow, and carries little weight!   1310
Come, see if you can't find some heavy line,
Something big and strong, to force the balance down!

EURIPIDES
Where can I find a line like that now, where?

DIONYSUS
"Achilles threw two aces and a four"?
Get ready to quote. This is the final round.

EURIPIDES
"And in his hand he held an iron-bound mace!"

AESCHYLUS
"Chariot lay piled on chariot, corpse on corpse!"

DIONYSUS
He's diddled you again!

EURIPIDES
                How did he do it?

DIONYSUS
He threw two chariots and two corpses in.
A hundred Egyptians couldn't lift that lot!   1320

AESCHYLUS

I'm tired of line-by-lines! Let him jump in the scale
Himself, and take his wife and children,
His ghost-writers and his book collection with him!
I'll weigh two lines of mine against the lot!

DIONYSUS

My friends, I simply can't decide between you!
I'd hate to make an enemy of either.
One's erudite, the other's entertaining.

PLUTO

You mean you've come down all this way for nothing?

DIONYSUS

And if I do decide?

PLUTO

                    You can take back
Whichever you choose, to repay you for your trouble.   1330

DIONYSUS

God bless you! Now come here and I'll explain.
I came down here to fetch a poet.

EURIPIDES

                    Why?

DIONYSUS

To save the city and keep up my worship.
So whichever of you seems to me to advise
The city best, that one I'll take with me.
First tell me what you think of Alcibiades.
All *our* ideas so far have been stillborn.

EURIPIDES

What does the city think of him?

DIONYSUS

                    The city?
She loves him, hates him, wants to have him back.
But tell me what *you* think about the man.   1340

EURIPIDES
I hate a man who's slow to help his country
And quick to harm it—who seeks his own advantage
But never lifts a finger for his city.

DIONYSUS
Well said. (*to* AESCHYLUS) What's your opinion of the man?

AESCHYLUS
Beware of rearing a lion in the city;
But if you have, then make the best of him.

DIONYSUS
So help me heaven, I still can't decide.
The one's intelligent, the other intelligible.
I'll put another question to you both.
What policy do you think best for Athens?   1350

EURIPIDES
I know, and am prepared to say.

DIONYSUS
                                        Speak up.

EURIPIDES
If we realize our allies are liars
And our liabilities are allies—

DIONYSUS
                                        Stop!
Say it again—less cleverly, more clearly.

EURIPIDES
If we distrust the citizens we've trusted
Up to this point, and trust the ones we haven't,
There's still some hope of safety for our city.
The present party's got us into trouble,
A change can only get us out of it.

DIONYSUS
Right on the button! What a brilliant mind!   1360
(*to* AESCHYLUS) And what do you say?

AESCHYLUS

First tell me about the city.
What citizens does she employ? The good ones?

DIONYSUS

No!

She hates them!

AESCHYLUS

Then you mean she likes the bad?

DIONYSUS
Not likes them; but she hasn't any choice.

AESCHYLUS (*rhetorically*)
What hope of safety is there for a city
When neither silk nor shoddy satisfies her?

DIONYSUS
You find one. That's the price of resurrection.

AESCHYLUS
I'll tell you when I've got there. Here I can't.

DIONYSUS
Oh no you don't! Send blessings from below.

AESCHYLUS
Then here it is: when she shall count her land   1370
Her enemies', and her enemies' land her own,
Her ships as treasure, money misery.

DIONYSUS
Well said! Though all the money goes in costs!

PLUTO
Make your decision!

DIONYSUS

This is how I'll do it;
I'll choose the man who gratifies my soul.

EURIPIDES
Remember all the gods by whom you swore

To take me back with you, and choose your friends!

DIONYSUS
It was only my tongue that swore—I'm choosing Aeschylus!

EURIPIDES
What have you done, you filthy traitor?

DIONYSUS
                              Me?
Given Aeschylus the prize. Why shouldn't I?   1380

EURIPIDES
Have you no shame? Can you look me in the face?

DIONYSUS
There's nothing shameful but the audience makes it so!

EURIPIDES
You devil! Do you mean to leave me dead?

DIONYSUS
Who knows if death be life, and life be death?
If breath be breakfast, sleep a pair of slippers?

(*Exit* EURIPIDES.)

PLUTO
Now, Dionysus, come in, both of you.

DIONYSUS
What for?

PLUTO
          I'll give a farewell breakfast for you.

DIONYSUS (*in tragic style*)
By Heaven, 'tis a plan most excellent!

(*Exeunt.*)

CHORUS
How blessed is intelligence!
You see it in every direction;   1390
For he by displaying good sense

Has won for himself resurrection.
Because of his wit he'll return to his city
The pride of his friends and relations,
And by counsel profound and sagacity sound
Bring blessings untold to the nation!

Let Socrates rattle his tongue,
You have more amusing resources;
While there's a good song to be sung
Why bother with ultimate causes?   1400
Philosophical rules are fit only for fools
While tragedy's got something in it,
So hold fast to your heart the commandments of art
And make the best use of each minute!

(*Enter* PLUTO, DIONYSUS *and* AESCHYLUS.)

PLUTO
Aeschylus, go on your way in peace,
And save our city by good advice;
And set up a school for fools—
There are plenty who need instruction! (*giving a whip*)
Take this gift to the democrats for me (*giving a club*)
And this to the Internal Revenue Commissioners (*giving a
    set of chains*)   1410
And this to all the graft-grabbing politicians.
Tell them to come down and pay me a visit,
And be quick about it; if they're slow
I'll come up myself and throw them in chains
And hurry them down below.

AESCHYLUS
I'll do as you wish. And as for my throne,
Let Sophocles keep it warm for me while I'm gone.
Perhaps some day I'll be back this way.
For he—and this is my firm conviction—
Is my true successor in poetic genius.   1420
But take care that no-good lying exhibitionist

Never gets a chance to sit on my throne,
Not even by accident!

PLUTO

My people, lift your holy torches high!
With the songs he wrote, with the music that he made,
Send him forward on his way in triumph!

(*The* CHORUS, PLUTO, DIONYSUS *and* AESCHYLUS *begin to file out in a grand procession.*)

CHORUS

Oh powers infernal, grant to our poet
Good journey as he goes forth to the light;
Grant that he give his land good counsel
And lead us back in the ways of right.   1430
Make us an end of the years of suffering,
Make us an end of the angry clash
Of arms; let the warmongers get together ·
And fight by themselves in their own cabbage patch!

NOTES

References are to line numbers

1 **Well master** . . . This opening scene demonstrates Aristophanes' ability to play to two sections of his audience at the same time. Xanthias' jokes represent the stock comic routines—the "Who's on first?" of Greek comedy. The Greek uses puns in which expressions ostensibly referring to the slave's heavy load of baggage can also be taken as references to the less mentionable bodily functions. American (though not English) "I'm loaded" has the same *double entendre*. While professing to mock such well-worn jokes, Aristophanes still contrives to bring most of them in, and so extracts a double laugh from one situation.

25 **I'm lifting things!** A more subtle parody, this time of current sophistic disputations on the correct use of grammar.

33 **. . . join the navy?** A reference to the battle of Arginousae, 406 B.C. Slaves who had fought in the battle were liberated. See Introduction, p. 126, and ll. 192 and 673.

47 **the old soft shoe** The buskin, a soft boot with slightly elevated sole and high uppers, traditional footwear of the tragic actor and worn here by Dionysus as god of tragedy. Dionysus' costume is deliberately ludicrous—like wearing a battledress with suède shoes and flowing cravat.

52 **"The Perils of Andromeda"** Euripides' *Andromeda*, now lost, was a stirring romantic melodrama in which the aerobatic hero rescued the princess from a sea-monster. For a more elaborate parody see Aristophanes' *Thesmophoriazousae*, ll. 1012 ff.

73 **the son of Sophocles** Iophon. Aristophanes later (l. 78) implies that he was plagiarizing his father's work.

84 **Agathon** A tragic poet of some eminence, none of whose work survives. Aristophanes elsewhere attacks his pretentiousness and effeminacy.

86 **the Happy Hunting Ground** The implication is that Agathon was as good as dead; like Euripides, he went to the court of King Archelaus of Macedonia, famous for its support of the arts.

87, 88 *Xenocles, Pythangelus*   inferior tragic poets.

101 *Conscience . . .*   Among the quotations from Euripides, Aristophanes includes a reminiscence of the notorious line from *Hippolytus* (428 B.C.) which could be taken as a defense of perjury (though Hippolytus does not in fact perjure himself in the play). Dionysus uses this line against Euripides to justify his eventual *volte-face* (l. 1378). That such a joke could still be made, twenty-three years after the initial performance, testifies to the retentiveness of the Athenian memory—though we must remember that they saw fewer plays than we do, and so remembered them more clearly.

110 *when you went to Hades*   One of Heracles' adventures had been the kidnapping of Cerberus, three-headed watchdog of the Underworld.

205 *unSalaminian*   A reference to the Greek naval victory over the Persians, 480 B.C.; or (less probably) to the state trireme *Salaminia*.

217 *As we sang in Athens. . . .*   The annual festival of Dionysus in Limnae, a place now unidentifiable.

333 *daughter of Demeter Persephone*   (see Introduction p. 130.)

350 *Or the man . . .*   Aristophanes reels off a list of contemporary nuisances. For a modern parallel see Ko-ko's song in *The Mikado*, with its refrain "I've got him on my list; He never will be missed" and the Mikado's "Make the punishment fit the crime" song in the same opera.

404 *Archedemus*   This and the two stanzas following could well be cut in modern performance. Archedemus, a politician of bad character, came into power 406/405. Cleisthenes was a notorious homosexual; in *Thesmophoriazousae* he is called in as the best judge of the true sex of a man in woman's disguise. Callias was a profligate youth of wealthy family who squandered his resources on riotous living.

598 *Take my slave . . .*   Under Greek and Roman law it was permissible to torture slaves to secure evidence. The beating scene which follows is a fine example of the way in which Aristophanes sacrifices logic to comic effect. As a genuine god,

Dionysus should be immune to pain, but it is much funnier to have both slave and master suffering equally.

661 *Cleophon*   Representative of the new type of politician whom Aristophanes satirizes freely. He was a man of the people, and a maker of musical instruments by profession. His mother was Thracian; his father seems to have been Athenian, but Aristophanes none the less satirizes him as an outlander who could not speak good Greek. The Athenians, fiercely proud of their pure and ancient blood, looked suspiciously on aliens.

667 *The chorus . . .*   Here we have the *parabasis*, a regular feature of Old Comedy. The chorus turns directly to the audience and addresses them on some matter of topical interest, often quite divorced from the action of the play. Comedy thus discharged one of its most important social functions, and could be a major force in influencing the public mind. Here they comment on a current abuse; slaves who had fought in one battle had been enfranchised, but citizens who had given the state years of service had lost the vote because of a trifling political misdemeanor.

687 *Cleigenes*   Another man of the people, one of Cleophon's most active supporters.

709 AEACUS   Some editors assign this part to an anonymous "SERVANT" on the grounds that the terrifying figure of the earlier scenes could not be the same as the genial character here. Aristophanes, however, has few qualms about making radical changes in characterization; and the scene could well be taken as a comic illustration of the theme of reconciliation just enunciated by the chorus.

785 *Imagine the roarer's implacable wrath*   This chorus summarizes the outstanding characteristics of the two playwrights. Aeschylus was noted for his grandiose style and vocabulary (the first three stanzas parody his elaborate word-formations) which even the next generation found hard to understand; Euripides, for his clever, epigrammatic style.

805 *The way he used to bluff us . . .*   see l. 884

810 *Uncircumlocutionary*   Euripides was given to prolixity and

circumlocution; here he criticizes Aeschylus for failing to display these qualities.

811 *child of the cabbage patch* Aristophanes never spares Euripides' family. His mother, according to a popular joke, kept a vegetable stall.

813 *pauper-poet* because Euripides represented so many beggars in his plays. His portrayal of low life in tragedy (see also "cripple-maker," l. 817, and passim) was one of the major accusations against him.

820 *lewd mimes and cancan dances* Euripides' exotic musical innovations were also held against him. The Greeks, like the Chinese, were great traditionalists in music; and we must remember that the musical score was a major part of tragedy.

826 *"Beggar Prince"* Euripides' *Telephus*, one of his most notorious plays, in which the princely hero was dressed as a beggar. *Telephus* was the *Hernani* or *Look Back in Anger* of its time; Aristophanes has only to mention the name to get a laugh.

834 *"Murderer at Large"*. . . . Euripides' *Peleus*, *Aeolus*, *Meleager*, and *Telephus* respectively, surviving now only in fragments but all sensational pieces in their time.

839 *My poetry didn't die with me* Aeschylus is wrong. Of the three tragedians, Euripides was by far the most popular after his death.

859 *Demeter* There is probably a joke here which we cannot fully appreciate. Aeschylus had been accused of revealing the secrets of the Eleusinian Mysteries, and only escaped punishment by proving that he was not an initiate himself.

865 *O air* . . . Euripides disdains the old gods and prays to the "deities" of rationalism. To "air" (more accurately *aether*, the upper air) which Euripides hails as the first principle of existence, we might compare Shaw's "Life Force."

883 *raised on blood and thunder* In the Greek text Aristophanes refers to Phrynichus, Aeschylus' predecessor, whose tragedies seem to have been colorful pageants without much spiritual content.

884 *a solitary character* A shrewd criticism. Aeschylus' trick of keeping characters silent to build up suspense (Cassandra in

Agamemnon, Pylades in *Libation-Bearers,* etc.) seems to have developed into a dramatic cliché.

886 *Four interminable stanzas* When Aeschylus wrote, the chorus was still the most important element in the drama, and his choruses are often of formidable length. Euripides placed more emphasis on the actors and allowed the chorus to fade into relative insignificance.

891 *wild and elephantine polysyllables* A hit at Aeschylus' fondness for weighty and archaic vocabulary.

904 *a capital offense* Aeschylus' objection is that low-life characters have no place on the tragic stage. Euripides counters with a political slogan: free speech for all! Dionysus' comment may be taken either to imply that such liberal views are dangerous, or that Euripides was by no means so democratic in his personal politics. Certainly his tragedies contain many expressions of sympathy with the aristocracy.

921 *True! Now every man . . .* Dionysus caps Euripides' peroration with a parody in the same meter (probably sung and danced) in which the tragedian's lofty principles are made ridiculous by being applied to the most humdrum of domestic incidents.

933 *Illustrious Achilles* A quotation from Aeschylus' lost *Myrmidons.* The implication is that Aeschylus, sulking under his rival's attacks, resembles the Homeric hero in his wrath against his colleagues.

952 *Good six-footers . . .* Aeschylus takes the position of a *laudator temporis acti.* Drama is a vital moral force in the state—both tragedians agree on this—and the nation's moral fiber has been weakened by Euripides' innovations.

956 *"The Seven Against Thebes"* Third and only surviving play on the misfortunes of the house of Oedipus. It deals with the civil war between Oedipus' sons, Eteocles and Polynices, and their deaths in mutual combat.

957 *So it's you . . .* The Thebans were enemies of Athens for most of the fifth century.

960 *"Persians"* produced in 472, our sole surviving example of a Greek tragedy on a topical subject. It relates, from the Persian viewpoint, the Greek naval victory at Salamis and the calamitous retreat of the Persian army.

961 *Yowoi* This exclamation does not occur in the extant text of the *Persians*. Some over-earnest critics have written it in; but Dionysus probably means only that the words of the chorus were unintelligible. The invocation of the ghost of Darius, late king of Persia, is one of the main scenes in the play.

962 *Consider how our poets . . .* Aeschylus gives a condensed history of Greek poetry. Orpheus and Musaeus were shadowy figures, supposedly pre-Homeric, the name of the former being associated with the mystical cult of Orphism. Hesiod wrote a manual of farming in verse, the *Works and Days*.

971 *hussies and adulterous entanglements* Euripides' misogynism was notorious (see the Introduction to *Medea*) and attributed by contemporary gossips to his unhappy married life. Much of this may be due to the ancient weakness for drawing inferences about a writer's life from his works (there is a similar tradition about Lucretius) but the joke in 974 implies that such slanders were common property during Euripides' lifetime.

984 *By costuming tragic kings . . .* Euripides made many innovations in stage practice, among them a new and more realistic style of costuming. His beggars, and kings in distress, were dressed in real rags—another practice felt to degrade the dignity of tragedy.

1035 *"Dark Hermes . . ."* Opening lines of the prologue to *The Libation-Bearers*, second play of the *Oresteia* trilogy. The quotation here helps us to reconstruct the prologue, mutilated in the surviving texts of the play.

1050 *He calls on Hermes . . .* Euripides justifiably calls attention to ambiguities in Aeschylus' expression. Whose father? Orestes' or Hermes'? Whose rights? Note how Dionysus interrupts this rather highbrow discussion with a silly joke (see Introduction, p. 121).

1078 *He came in secret . . .* In *The Libation-Bearers* Orestes, returning to his homeland to avenge his father's murder, has to enter the country in secret and disguise himself to gain access to his ancestral house.

1092 *"A happy man . . ."* Opening line of Euripides' *Antigone*, now lost.

1105 *All he needed* . . . A further allusion to the battle of Arginousae (see Introduction p. 126).

1110 *I'll take an oil-can* . . . Much has been written about this, the most famous scene in the whole comedy. Critics have labored to find esoteric significance in the oil-can joke. It has been suggested that Aristophanes is parodying Euripides' excessive use of domestic detail in his tragedies, or his increasingly elaborate resolutions of the standard iambic line into collocations of short syllables. Neither of these explanations is entirely convincing. It is perhaps safer to take the whole scene as ingenious nonsense. The device of capping a serious line with an irrelevant, though syntactically appropriate, tag is a familiar form of humor. We find it in Molière, in Elizabethan drama, in television comedy. The present scene is glorious verbal farce. Euripides' quotations are from his *Archelaus, Hypsipyle, Sthenoboia, Phrixos, Iphigeneia in Tauris, Meleager* and *Melanippe the Wise* respectively. Only *Iphigeneia* survives.

1174 *"Achilles, can you hear the shock . . ."* The point must remain partly obscure, as we have neither Aeschylus' music nor that of Aristophanes, and so cannot see how in this most important respect the parody compares with the original. Nevertheless, Euripides clearly indicates that he finds his rival's lyrics monotonous, and emphasizes this by introducing the same refrain after each line. The verses quoted are from *Ghost-Raisers, Telephus* or *Iphigeneia, Priestesses* and *Agamemnon*, of which only the last play survives. Once again Dionysus cuts off a promising discussion with a coarse joke.

1192 *I'll tell how* . . . A Lewis Carroll-like jumble of lines from *Agamemnon* and *Sphinx*, making a kind of mad sense.

1216 *Sweet is the squawk* . . . If Aeschylus could be accused of monotony, Euripides could be accused of wildness and irregularity in his verse-structures. Aeschylus replies in kind by presenting a similar farrago of Euripidean lyrics chosen from various sources. 1221 contains a typical Euripidean trill.

1241 *O sable night* . . . Here the point is clearer. Aristophanes is satirizing content rather than form. Aeschylus' parody has two targets: Euripides use of the mundane and commonplace in tragedy, and his weakness for supernatural effects. A simple domestic tale of a servant-girl who steals her mistress' cockerel is wrapped in the guise of high tragedy, with the appearance of a foreboding ghost, a ritual purification, the disaster itself and the invocation of the avenging gods.

1279 *to bring him to the balance*   Here the comedy abandons all pretense of serious literary criticism. Lines are judged by their physical weight. Euripides, though he eventually catches on (l. 1316), cannot compete against Aeschylus. The lines are from *Medea, Philoctetes; Antigone, Niobe; Telephus* (l. 1314) and *Meleager, Glaukos Potnieus*. Only *Medea* survives.

1336 *Alcibiades*   See Introduction, p. 127. This unpredictable genius, having fought on both sides in the Peloponnesian War, was now in voluntary exile in Thrace.

1345 *a lion in the city*   i.e. a creature harmless at first but dangerous when full-grown. In *Agamemnon* ll. 717 ff. Aeschylus uses the metaphor of Helen.

1397 *Socrates*   satirized by Aristophanes in *The Clouds*, and classed together with Euripides by the popular mind as an eccentric intellectual.